LEADING Life-Changing SMALL GROUPS

The WILLOW CREEK Guide to

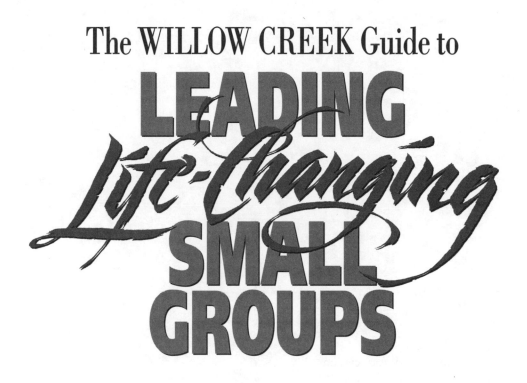

LEADING Life-Changing SMALL GROUPS

Bill Donahue

ZondervanPublishingHouse
Grand Rapids, Michigan

A Division of HarperCollinsPublishers

WILLOW CREEK

RESOURCES™

Leading Life-Changing Small Groups
Copyright © 1996 by the Willow Creek Association

Requests for information should be addressed to:

📖 ZondervanPublishingHouse
Grand Rapids, Michigan 49530

Library of Congress Cataloging-in-Publication Data

Donahue, Bill.
   Leading life-changing small groups / Bill Donahue.
      p.   cm.
   Rev. ed. of: Willow Creek small groups. ©1994.
   Includes bibliographical references (p.   ) and index.
   ISBN: 0-310-20595-6 (softcover)
   1.Church group work. 2. Small groups. I. Donahue, Bill. Willow Creek small groups. II. Willow Creek Community
Church (South Barrington, Ill.) III. Title.
BV652.2.D66   1996
253'.7—dc 20
                                                             96-17624
                                                                  CIP

Edited by Jack Kuhatschek and Rachel Boers
Interior design by Mark Veldheer

Printed in the United States of America

---

00 01 02 03 /❖ PC/ 20 19

Contents

Part 1: Small Group Philosophy

Section 1—Vision and Values

Section 2—Structure

Section 3—Resources

Part 2: The Making of a Leader

Section 1—Biblical Leadership

Section 2—Leadership Responsibilities

Part 3: Developing Apprentice Leaders

Part 4: Group Life

Part 5: Conducting Meetings

Part 6: Shepherding Members

Part 7: Multiplying Your Ministry

Part 8: Starting Small Groups in Your Church

This handbook is dedicated to the volunteer ministers of Willow Creek who invest their time, talents, and resources to shepherd, care for, disciple, and lead the members of small groups toward maturity in Christ. May Christ reward you for your faithful service and unwavering devotion to your ministry.

Foreword

Willow Creek's well-deserved reputation for excellence is not limited to its celebration arts and seeker-targeted services. When Bill Hybels surveyed the new generation of seekers and believers thronging to the Willow Creek campus, he took responsibility for assuring that they would be welcomed, instructed, and cared for. He led by casting a vision for top leadership and staff to do whatever it took to multiply the number of volunteer spiritual shepherds.

In this excellent volume, Bill Donahue and team share the training philosophy that translates Pastor Hybels' vision of assuring care into a daily reality at Willow Creek Community Church.

Now, over a thousand lay ministers at Willow Creek lead small groups and serving teams where a well-trained and supervised lay leader knows each person by name. Whether called together by the lay ministers for Bible study, a special interest, or a serving assignment, these thousands of emerging disciples experience a quality of caring that most Christians can only wish for.

Carl F. George

Preface

Welcome. This manual has been designed for small groups by small groups. It is a reference guide for your ministry, providing all the information and resources you need to lead an effective and dynamic small group . . . the kind in which life change is the norm, not the exception.

You'll find that *Leading Life-Changing Small Groups* is organized in a way that makes it easy for you to find the information you need when you need it. It is also designed with a lot of common sense in mind. Each section naturally leads to the next. And you will use certain parts of it time after time as you forge ahead to lead the kind of small group that turns participants into fully devoted followers of Jesus Christ.

▶ How This Guide Is Designed

The introduction to this book, titled "A Structure That Serves People," describes some of the basic workings of a small group strategy I have found to be very successful—a strategy based on Carl George's meta-church model for small groups. You'll discover how the meta-church model is designed, how it is used, and why it is effective. Please take time to read the introduction, as it provides a basic foundation for the rest of the book.

Part 1 begins with the underlying biblical principles and values of a successful small group ministry. What people believe—really believe—gives rise to their actions. What you believe about Christian community, evangelism, discipleship, and the role of small groups in the body of Christ will determine the impact of your ministry efforts. This section provides you with the core for developing a thriving and exciting ministry.

Part 2 strikes at the heart of a successful small group: leadership. Several trained, gifted, and passionate leaders form the backbone of a small group ministry intent on developing fully devoted and fruitful Christ followers. The spiritual life of the small group leader, a small group leader's job description, and the character of the shepherd of a little flock are all addressed in this section.

Part 3 focuses on the successful multiplication of leaders through the process of apprenticing. Leadership development is not the responsibility of a few paid staff members. It is the privilege of every small group leader to identify, challenge, motivate, and equip people who will then develop into leaders of life-changing groups.

Part 4 draws your attention to the life and vitality of the small group. Once you have developed vision and values to guide your ministry, derived a clear understanding of your role as a leader in the body of Christ, and committed to the identification and mentoring of other potential leaders, you can begin to put together a dynamic group. Forming groups, setting the group vision, and establishing a covenant of commitment based on shared values is the focus of this section.

Part 5 walks you through the skills and information needed to conduct life-changing meetings—from planning a meeting to using great questions, handling basic conflicts, building relationships, leading dynamic discussions, and gaining feedback on the group and your leadership.

Part 6 helps the leader become a shepherd. That's what you are: a shepherd-leader—someone who provides a sense of vision and direction for the group, who encourages members toward Christlikeness, and who facilitates dynamic meetings where the Word of God is understood, reflected upon, and obeyed. But a leader also helps the group become a caring, nurturing environment where members find rest for their souls, prayer for their needs, and healing for their wounds. As a shepherd, your little flock deserves your attention and insight.

Part 7 is designed to help you multiply your ministry. As a leader, you have the privilege of extending the kingdom of God beyond the group and of reaching out to others who have yet to experience the fullness of true community in Christ. You'll learn how to invite other sheep into the fold, how to bring them into the life-giving environment of your group, and how to assist your rising leaders to step out and begin to lead groups of their own.

Part 8 shows you how to get small groups started in your church and provides a method for evaluating the effectiveness of a small group ministry. The processes and steps outlined here will help new ministries get off to a great start and allow existing ministries to take stock of themselves, making the necessary changes and improvements to move their efforts to new and exciting levels of growth and Christlikeness.

I appreciate the hard work of all those who participated in the creation of this handbook, but a special note of thanks should go to Debbie Beise, Cindi Salazar, Judson Poling, and Todd Wendorff for their contributions. Without their hard work and commitment, we would not have this valuable resource for leaders.

Thanks also to Carl George for providing the church with a ministry model that is life-giving and that works! Your contribution to the kingdom will bear fruit for generations to come.

Bill Donahue

A Structure That Serves People

Structure can facilitate or impede the ministry efforts of any group, large or small. Churches and small groups often fail to link the ideals and enthusiasm for vital Christian ministry with an organizational design that allows ministry to flourish. But how does a church know when the design of a group or large organization encourages ministry or frustrates it? Let's answer that question with a question. Does the structure serve the people, or do the people serve the structure?

Many organizations (and many small groups) unknowingly create a system that views people as resources to fuel the organization. Sadly, some churches motivate members with guilt or spiritualized manipulation in order to get them to fill a volunteer slot in the organization. "Our children will drift through life without direction and purpose, wandering dangerously close to the abyss of carnality, unless you sign up to teach in the children's ministry today!"

Small groups—and small group leaders—commit the same error. Leaders protest, "I worked on this lesson for seven hours. It's not fair to me when you don't do the assignment. All my work goes to waste!" Translation: "I worked hard to create something you ought to listen to. Because I created it, you should want to hear it. After all, you exist to provide an audience for my teaching and leading skills. If you don't do your part, how am I ever going to have a ministry?"

Such appeals may have an element of truth in them, but in both cases it is assumed that the people exist to serve the organization's needs. Rather, the organization must be designed to serve the *people* the church is called to shepherd and disciple. The meta-church model we have adopted and refined throughout this manual presents an organizational strategy with a view toward the empowerment and development of people. Small group leaders, eager to help their people to be faithful servants and fruitful stewards of the gifts God has given them, will discover that this ministry structure empowers their leadership while effectively freeing their members for ministry and service in the body of Christ and in the world around them.

▶ Key Components of the Meta-Church Strategy for Groups

The term *meta* means "change." A meta-church is a church that is changing the way it accomplishes the expansion of the kingdom. A meta-church is organized around cell groups, where people can find friendship, be mentored in the faith, understand and discuss the truth of the Word, identify and use their spiritual gifts, and provide care for one another. (For more information about how such churches are organized, refer to Carl George's books *Prepare Your Church for the Future* and *The Coming Church Revolution*.)

Span of care

It is impossible for a pastor to provide attention, discipleship, and care needed for large groups of people. No one has the time and energy to shepherd a flock of 80 or 200 or 500 people. So what is a reasonable span of care? We recommend a ratio of 1:10—for every leader team, up to ten members can be cared for. As a volunteer leader in the church, your time is limited. Shepherding a group of six to ten people is a challenging yet manageable flock.

A church's ability to provide a personal touch is often lost as it grows. A smaller church of 65 that reaches 30 people for Christ must now assimilate these people, nurture them in the faith, and provide ongoing care for their personal needs. Perhaps a few key volunteers and a paid pastor could accomplish this task when there were 65 members. But now with 95 members (and so many new babes in Christ who need attention) it is necessary for the caregiving to be shared by many, rather than a few. Ten small groups with apprentice leaders would make this church a more vital, caring, and personal place. With no one caring for more than ten (including the paid pastor who would primarily train and shepherd the small group leaders and devote more of his time to the preaching of the Word and prayer as in Acts 6:4), each person would feel cared for.

Leadership development

Turning fully devoted followers into fully developed leaders is both difficult and rewarding. It is difficult because it requires focus, energy, and persistence. Leadership development will never cry out, "This must have your undivided attention today!" Such cries come from sermon preparation, music practice, staff conflicts, building programs, finance committee meetings, pastoral counseling, and dissident members. We all know we need more qualified and trained leaders, but leadership development can always wait until next week, or until we "get over this hump," or finish the addition, or when the staff has some extra time. In other words, never.

Your group, and the small group ministry at your church, thrives on the ability to identify and develop qualified leaders to shepherd little flocks of believers and reach out to strays who need Christ. Without this ministry, the church will die. In the meta-church model, leadership development is intentionally pursued by the small group leader and pastoral staff. Leaders, working with the support and direction of staff, identify potential leaders and make an effort to disciple them in the direction of small group leadership. Each group consists of an active leader, at least one apprentice leader learning the ropes of small group leadership while on the job, and a host/hostess who will provide an environment conducive to a dynamic group experience. The meta-church model also encourages the leader to identify new, rising leaders—leaders who have potential, but who are not yet prepared for any formal role. Once identified, these rising leaders are challenged by the active leader to become apprentices.

No group should begin without a leadership team in place. This ensures that leadership is being shared and developed, and demonstrates how serious the church is about the future of the ministry. Groups that start without apprentices or rising leaders will become ingrown and unable to produce new group life. The small group is an ideal place for rising leaders to experiment with their spiritual gifts, gain feedback from the group, be coached by the leader, and grow into leadership.

Group multiplication

Speak to your average small group leaders about multiplication, and they often react with fear. "Don't break up our group!" cry most leaders. But the kingdom of God advances one life at a time. We are called to multiply our ministry by extending the kingdom and enfolding new followers. The use of the open chair to allow for consistent, well-paced group growth will enable new believers or inquiring seekers to find a group. And the intentional development of apprentice leaders ensures that someone will be ready to lead new groups as existing groups grow and give birth to new life. As new groups form from existing ones, the values and principles learned can be multiplied.

Everyone needs a place to experience community. Excitement and enthusiasm arise as lives change and new people enter into meaningful relationships in community. It is natural that groups will form subgroups made up of three to four people each. These subgroups can, in turn, develop leaders, add members, and ultimately separate into their own healthy groups. The process continues until everyone who wants community finds a little flock that will take them in, grow them up, and release them for ministry.

Relational discipleship

The best discipleship is group discipleship. Jesus practiced it, spending much of His time with no fewer than three of the twelve disciples. Group learning and ministry experiences have distinct advantages. People who are discipled in the context of a small group experience benefit from the wisdom and discernment of many group members, are able to use their gifts in a safe and encouraging setting, can have needs met and prayed for by several brothers and sisters in Christ, and can be encouraged toward team ministry. One-on-one meetings and mentoring are enhanced by the broader group experience, and the leader is protected from bearing the entire disciplemaking responsibility. Thus we "bear one another's burdens" and engage in mutual ministry in the body of Christ.

Turning irreligious people into fully devoted followers of Christ has always been at the heart of God and His church. Jesus commanded us to speak, love, and serve others as He would, and live lives that are increasing in love, joy, and the other fruit of the Spirit. Disciples are not just people with more answers to Bible questions or who attend more events or listen to more Christian radio. Disciples are people who act like Christ, who are willing to train to be like Him, who practice the disciplines of prayer, solitude, worship, Bible reading and study, community, and ministry. They are lifelong learners and lovers of Christ. Small groups that get intentional about this will see fruit multiplied in people's lives.

Ministry coordination

Churches, regardless of size, often function as a collection of parachurch ministries that just happen to have the same address. They share facilities, resources, volunteers, finances, and scriptural mandates, but you'll be hard-pressed to find them actually working together toward common goals and purposes. The meta-church model is a "whole church" model that fosters teamwork and coordination of ministry efforts. Since all ministries of the church are designed and developed using small groups, it is essential that all of those groups function together to accomplish the church's mission. Since the meta-church model employs the same small group structure for all ministries of the church (youth, children, choir, adult ministries, international outreach, et cetera), that structure provides a common delivery system for ministry throughout the organization.

For example, a church might determine to rally the troops around the goal of reaching their community for Christ. In addition to the preaching and teaching ministries that challenge and exhort the people, small groups can become a place where evangelism skills are modeled and practiced, prayer and support are provided, accountability is enhanced, and the assimilation of newly reached followers occurs. Small group leaders throughout the church can be brought together for training, feedback, vision casting, and prayer. Regardless of the size and scope of their particular ministry, each one can "own" the mission of reaching the community and can articulate it to their small group members. This is an effective strategy for churches of 80, 800, or 8,000.

▶ Questions You Must Answer When Designing a Ministry Structure

1. *Will we be a church* with *small groups or a church* of *small groups?* Make sure you can answer this question with clarity, for it will determine your ministry for the next several years. If your church has small groups but does not want to organize its ministry around small groups, then "small groups" is *a program or department* of the church. It is optional.

However, if you have chosen to accomplish ministry together in little communities, then "small groups" *is* the church. Groups provide a delivery system for truth, disciplemaking, and caregiving. They represent much of the body life of the church. This means that *all* staff and board members will model group life and participate in furthering the vision for groups. It will not be the responsibility of one staff member alone to implement and assume responsibility for a group-based ministry.

2. *How will we determine what an appropriate span of care is for our staff and for our volunteers?* A church's ministry structure determines who is responsible to provide nurture and development to others in the structure, from senior pastor to the church board to church members. After setting priorities, allocating time, and expending resources and energy, determine what is available for a small groups ministry. Remember, there are limitations to what any one person can do. If everyone must be cared for, and no one should care for more than ten, then design your spans of care accordingly, doing all you can to honor those spans.

3. *Can structure be adapted to accommodate change?* Changes in ministry needs, numbers of members, limitations in facilities and parking, educational priorities, and the church's strategy are inevitable. Because of this, it is important that your structure not be rigid. It must allow for the deployment of resources and people in such a way that the vitality of ministry is never compromised. The structure of a small group must always enhance the ministry, not impede its progress.

4. *What will be the roles of staff and volunteers?* Are the ministries of the paid staff esteemed more highly than the ministries of the unpaid? Will paid staff concern themselves with the identification, training, and development of the body of Christ? Structures must empower, release, and support the ministry of members in the body. Small groups that release people for ministry but fail to empower or support them are allowing that ministry to falter. Volunteers who feel ill-equipped

and isolated soon burn out and move on. Only when the right structure is coupled with the right philosophy of ministry will it yield the desired results.

The meta-church strategy addresses these issues with clarity. It is an approach to ministry that is effective and understandable. It is not without weaknesses or problems—no strategy or structure could make that claim. But because the meta-church strategy is so clearly defined and articulated, church leaders are able to exploit its strengths and accommodate adequately for its weaknesses.

The remainder of this book is devoted to helping you put this strategy to work in the life of the local church.

▶ Part One

Small Group Philosophy

Vision and Values

Mission Statement and Ministry Philosophy for Small Groups

A mission statement and ministry philosophy are key to the success of your ministry because they function as navigational tools necessary to chart an accurate course toward a worthy destination. The mission and philosophy statement used to launch small group ministry of Willow Creek Community Church in South Barrington, Illinois, serve as an example. Below, and on the following pages, you'll find this mission and ministry philosophy outlined and explained. As you read it, consider how you might shape and articulate *your* church's vision and values.

The overriding mission at Willow Creek is to "turn irreligious people into fully devoted followers of Christ." In order to accomplish that mission, a variety of ministries exist at Willow Creek. From the weekend service to the midweek New Community believer's service to the various subministries throughout Willow Creek, we are committed to moving people toward Christlikeness. Since small groups have become our way of doing ministry, it is essential that we understand the role they play in carrying out our overall mission.

Below, you will notice the mission statement for the purpose of small groups at Willow Creek and how small groups are used to accomplish our overriding mission. The questions "Why do small groups exist?" and "For what purpose do

Mission Statement

"To connect people relationally in groups (four to ten individuals) for the purpose of growing in Christlikeness, loving one another, and contributing to the work of the church, in order to glorify God and make disciples of all nations."

small groups exist?" are answered in the mission statement. Following the mission statement you will find a philosophy of ministry structured around five key statements we believe will shape the way Willow Creek does ministry for the coming years. These five statements are strategic assumptions, based on Scripture, that undergird our ministry philosophy.

▶ Our Mandate

Jesus Christ, as Head of the church, intends His followers to become like Him

It is God's plan that those who call on His name should be like Him in attitude and behavior. The church exists not just to collect the saints, but to transform them.

Church life is the sum of all the activities that promote Christ's work of transformation. Programs and subministries in a church should be designed to serve His goal of changing lives, and should be surrendered as obsolete when they fail to achieve this end.

We describe the life change the church exists to produce with "The Five G's": *Grace* (the individual appropriation of the saving work of Christ), *Growth* (the ongoing evidence of a changing life and pursuit of Christlikeness), *Group* (connection with others in significant relationships), *Gifts* (serving Christ's body according to spiritual giftedness and passion), and *Good stewardship* (honoring God with our resources through what we give to the church and what we keep).

The Five G's				
Grace	*Growth*	*Group*	*Gifts*	*Good Stewardship*

▶ Our Method

A small group provides the optimal environment for the life change Jesus Christ intends for every believer

Significant relationships (including one-to-one) occur best in the context of a small group. Connecting people in a small group is not an optional subministry of the church—it *is* the church in its smallest unit. Without this connection, people can, at best, attend meetings, but they aren't truly participating in church.

A small group of believers who love one another with God's love will experience the life Christ promised at the deepest level possible. This love radically transforms them and demonstrates His power. A group that by design does not contribute to this goal of spiritual maturity may well be a collection of Christians, but it is not a successful small group.

A variety of small groups are necessary to meet the individual needs of believers, as well as the diverse needs of the body as a whole. People can grow in Christlikeness, care for each other, and make a contribution in any group, whether it be a disciplemaking group, task group, nurture group, Christian twelve-step group, counseling group, or any other type. However, ministries in a local church that

---

"...*I have set you an example that you should do as I have done for you.*"

John 13:15

Other Scriptures:
    John 14:15
    Romans 6:12–13, 17–19;
      8:29
    Philippians 1:6
    Colossians 1:28; 2:6–7
    1 John 2:6

"*He appointed twelve— designating them apostles—that they might be with him.*"

Mark 3:14

Other Scriptures:
    Exodus 18:17–27
    Acts 2:46

don't have small groups built into their structure generally can't produce optimal life change for people looking to that ministry for growth and service opportunities.

►Our Model

The most strategic person in the life-change process of the church is the small group leader

The priority of church leadership is to help small group leaders succeed through support and training. To that end, the best resources of the church should be employed to make sure the small group leader has everything necessary for effectiveness.

Small group leaders cannot flourish in a vacuum. Leaders need to band together periodically with other leaders for encouragement and accountability (huddling). Additionally, church staff and other leaders must provide training in skills necessary for group life (skill training) and reminders of the purpose and goals that drive the ministry (vision casting). Basic skills necessary for effective leadership of a small group are the same whether one is leading a task group of volunteers, a youth team, or a few people in a disciplemaking small group.

Leaders need oversight from coaches who can offer them encouragement and accountability. Coaches should not violate an appropriate span of care (1:10). This ratio holds true throughout the entire church—everyone must be cared for by someone, and no one should care for more than ten people.

The ultimate goal of a leader is life change: to help group members grow in Christlike character through learning, loving one another, and contributing of themselves and their resources. Yet leaders must also help their groups grow in size and eventually birth new groups. (We acknowledge that some groups are closed to address specific issues or cover a specific curriculum.) The leader takes responsibility for this growth by recruiting an apprentice, attending training, and by planning for the eventual birthing process.

►Our Mechanism

Groups must expand and multiply so that eventually every believer can be connected to others

A small group does not ultimately exist for itself. Christlike people resist the urge to be selfish—they desire to include other unconnected people in such a way that they too may experience group life. Small groups therefore must have a viable strategy for growth and reproduction so that someday everyone who gathers as a part of the local church is included in some kind of identifiable relational connection.

An apprentice program to foster new leaders must be an integral part of group life so that emerging leaders continually gain on-the-job experience and can be ready to lead groups of their own as soon as they are ready.

When a group gets too large, its leader cannot provide the care necessary for life transformation of each individual. Though groups must grow, the appropriate span

"It was he who gave some to be apostles, some to be prophets, some to be evangelists, and some to be pastors and teachers, to prepare God's people [average believers] for works of service."
Ephesians 4:11–12

Other Scriptures:
1 Corinthians 16:15–16
1 Thessalonians 5:12–13
Hebrews 13:7, 17

"And the things you have heard me say . . . entrust to reliable men who will also be qualified to teach others."
2 Timothy 2:2

Other Scriptures:
Matthew 9:36–38;
29:19–20
Acts 1:8

of care of approximately one leader for every ten people needs to be maintained. The next step for groups that grow above ten members is to birth new groups.

Success in leadership of a small group is ultimately seen in the viability of daughter groups. The goal is not just to start a new group, but to birth a group that is healthy and creates life change. The new group can only be considered viable if it eventually births a new group itself. In this model, a senior leader is someone who's birthed additional groups, which in turn have birthed new groups—in other words, a leader with small group "grandchildren."

▶ Our Means

Effective ministry happens in an atmosphere of prayer and celebration

> "And the disciples were filled with joy and with the Holy Spirit."
>
> Acts 13:52
>
> *Other Scriptures:*
> Nehemiah 8:9–12
> Acts 2:46–47; 8:4–8
> Luke 10:17, 21

God is sovereign, and He sovereignly declares that we should pray. Great ministry follows great praying—believers who talk to their heavenly Father receive because they ask; when they knock, He opens. Leaders are to pray as Jesus prayed: publicly as well as privately, authentically as well as powerfully, specifically as well as continually. Those who seek God's blessing on their work must seek His presence in their work through prayer.

God's activity must be noticed, shared, valued, and celebrated. A climate of fun and festivity should permeate gatherings related to ministries.

Leadership successes should be a source of public as well as private rejoicing. Small group gatherings do not take the place of many people coming together for public exaltation of God, teaching of His Word, and calling attention to what He is doing among the members of the church in small groups. What happens at the small group level should happen at the large gathering, and vice versa.

Developing Fully Devoted Followers

The ultimate purpose of small groups is to move people toward a greater relationship with Christ and to transform people into His image. But often the question is asked, "What does it mean to be like Jesus?" Below, you'll find some teaching on discipleship, and then you will see how we define a disciple of Christ in terms of the local church. As you read, think first about your own development as a disciple. Then, decide how you will function as a Christ follower in your local assembly.

▶ What Is a Disciple?

In the simplest form, a disciple is a follower and learner of Jesus Christ

> "A student is not above his teacher, nor a servant above his master. It is enough for the student to be like his teacher, and the servant like his master."
>
> Matthew 10:24–25

At Willow Creek we define discipleship as "living as Christ would if He were in my place." Discipleship—in these broad terms—implies a life of transformation and continued yieldedness to the Holy Spirit.

▶ How Does a Disciple Function in the Local Church?

We have now expanded on that definition of a disciple by describing the function of a disciple in and through the local church. As one functions as a Christ-follower in the local church, one becomes a "participating member" of that local body. A participating member at Willow Creek (that is, a Christ follower or disciple) is described as one who is maturing in the following five areas.

Grace

Christ followers understand and have individually received Christ's saving grace. They have abandoned all attempts to earn God's favor through accomplishments of their own and find security only through Christ's sacrificial death on their behalf.

In obedience to Christ's command, they have undergone water baptism as believers, giving outward witness to the inner cleansing and renewal experienced in Him.

The individual appropriation of the saving work of Christ.

Ephesians 2:8–9

Growth

Christ followers know that the grace of God that saved them is only the beginning of His work in them. They gratefully respond by actively pursuing a lifelong process of spiritual growth in Christ and by seeking to become conformed to His image. To this end, they consistently nurture their spiritual development through prayer, worship, and Bible study.

They regard the Bible as the final authority in all areas that it teaches about and desire to be wholly obedient to it. Christ followers honestly confront areas of personal sin and engage the Holy Spirit's power in seeking to turn from sin.

Christ followers also desire to extend the grace they've received to others through personal evangelism and participation in the collective ministry of the church in their community, their country, and around the world.

The ongoing evidence of a changing life in pursuit of Christlikeness.

2 Peter 3:18

Group

A Christ follower honors God's call to participate in community in order to grow in Christlikeness, express and receive love, and carry out the ministry of the church.

For this reason, Christ followers give priority to attending the corporate gatherings of the church for the purpose of worship, teaching, and participation in the sacrament of communion, and are connected relationally to a small group of believers for the purpose of mutual encouragement, support, and accountability.

Christ followers also

- pursue Christ-honoring relationships at home, within the church, and in the marketplace, and are committed to pursuing the biblical pattern of reconciliation when conflict arises;

- support the leadership of the church and are biblically submissive to it;

- affirm and uphold the fundamental truths of Scripture (as summarized in our Statement of Faith) and refrain from promoting other doctrines in ways that cause dissension.

Connections with others in significant relationships.

Acts 2:46

Serving Christ's body according to spiritual giftedness and passion.

         Romans 12:6–8

Honoring God financially through what we give to the church and what we keep.

         Philippians 4:11–19

Gifts

Christ followers recognize that the church is composed of interdependent members, each uniquely gifted by the Holy Spirit for the purpose of building up the body and furthering the ministry of the church. They therefore seek to discover, develop, and deploy those God-given gifts and to seek a place of service within the church with the support and affirmation of the body.

Good stewardship

Christ followers realize they have been bought with the price of Christ's blood, and that everything they are and have belongs to Him.

In light of this, they desire to be responsible caretakers of the material resources with which God has entrusted them. They recognize the tithe (ten percent of one's earnings) as the historical standard of giving in Scripture. But, moreover, in response to Christ's abundant giving, they increasingly submit their resources to His lordship and display a spirit of generosity and cheerfulness in supporting the work of the church and reaching out, with compassion, to a need world.

Small Groups in the New Testament

Community is a theme that runs throughout Scripture. God has always been calling out a people for Himself, beginning with Israel and continuing with the church. Even when the Jews were dispersed among enemy nations during times of captivity, they organized themselves into groups and ultimately formed synagogues (Jewish communities of worship and teaching), where they could serve one another and carry out their beliefs. It was natural, therefore, for Jesus to develop a community of followers and for Paul, Peter, and other church planters to start new communities wherever they went as they proclaimed the Gospel. These new communities began as small groups, just as Jesus had modeled with the twelve disciples (Mark 3:14; Luke 6:12–19).

Small groups were an integral part of the early church structure. They were small enough to allow individual members to minister to one another, use their spiritual gifts, and be discipled in the teachings of Christ. In addition, they were vibrant and life-giving communities where evangelism could take place as unchurched people watched a loving and compassionate community in action. Small groups not only built up the church but were vehicles for reaching a lost world for Christ.

What Is Biblical Community?

Believers in Christ are called to live in mutually accountable relationships as they reflect the loving character of God, walk in step with the Spirit, and build up the church in order to proclaim the Good News to the world.

Definition of Biblical Community:

"Christian Community is the body of Christ expressing the life and message of Christ to build up one another and redeem the world for God's glory."

▶ Key Scriptures About Community in the New Testament

The new community that formed on the Day of Pentecost immediately began to function in small groups. These groups wholeheartedly devoted themselves to the teaching of the apostles, to fellowship with one another, to practicing the Lord's Supper together, and to praying for one another. These new communities were characterized by mutuality, accountability, servanthood, love, and evangelism.

Small groups are a place of mutual ministry among members. Each member uses spiritual gifts to serve other members in the body. Mutual ministry is a trademark of a Christ-following community or small group.

A small group gathers together to provide fellowship and mutual support so that the church can have an impact in society. They encourage and build up one another so that the body of Christ can be cared for and the world can be influenced through their good deeds.

Small groups exist to teach the truth and develop future leaders who can shepherd others and disciple them in the faith. For this purpose, each leader, or coach, has an apprentice he or she is developing toward greater responsibility and leadership.

"Every day they continued to meet together in the temple courts. They broke bread in their homes and ate together with glad and sincere hearts, praising God and enjoying the favor of all the people."

Acts 2:46–47

"Now to each one the manifestation of the Spirit is given for the common good."

1 Corinthians 12:7

"And let us consider how we may spur one another on toward love and good deeds. Let us not give up meeting together, as some are in the habit of doing, but let us encourage one another—and all the more as you see the Day approaching."

Hebrews 10:24–25

"And the things you have heard me say ... entrust to reliable men who will also be qualified to teach others."

2 Timothy 2:2

Structure

Structure of Small Groups

A variety of small groups have been developed to accommodate the many needs and levels of maturity of attenders of a local church. Groups typically form around areas of affinity such as marital status, age, ministry, task, personal need, life stage, et cetera. Though we recognize the autonomy and distinctiveness of each individual small group, most groups can be characterized as one of the five listed below.

Five Major Types of Groups

	Disciple-Making Groups	Community Groups	Service Groups	Seeker Groups	Support Groups
Members	Believers seeking a structured disciple-ship process	Believers and nonbelievers	Believers and nonbelievers	Predominantly nonbelievers	Believers and nonbelievers
Curriculum	A set curriculum such as the *Walking with God* series by Zondervan	Leaders work with Coaches to choose curriculum	Leaders work with Coaches to choose curriculum	Determined by questions of members	Determined by ministry leaders
Open Chair	Used at breaks in curriculum	Used regularly to add members	Used regularly to add members	Always has an open chair	Used primarily to form new groups
Emphasis	Develop spiritual disciplines, memorize Scripture, disciple others	Build community, invite new members	Complete the task, invite new members	Lead people to Christ, disciple new converts	To support members as they work through personal difficulties
Multiplication	Apprentice leads new disciple-making group	Groups grow and birth after 24-36 meetings	Groups grow and birth at variable rates depending on the task	Apprentice leads new seeker group or new believers group	Apprentices are trained to form new groups
Duration	18-24 months	Continue to grow and birth	Continue to grow and birth	Average length is about one year	Varies depending upon personal needs and purpose of group

A Typical Community Group

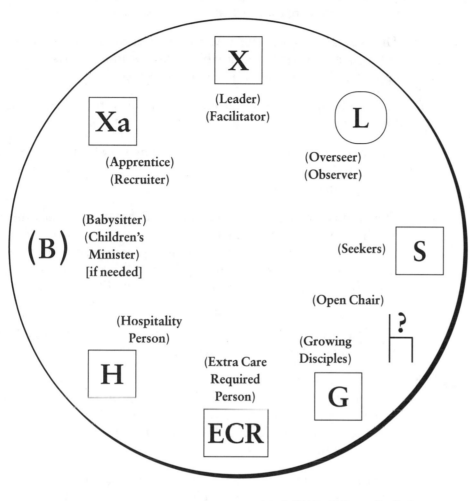

© 1991 Carl F. George, Used by Permission

Above you see a picture of the average community group. As mentioned earlier, we use a small group model pioneered by Carl George and described in his book *Prepare Your Church for the Future.* The group diagrammed above represents the typical small group in George's model. Certainly not all groups have the makeup of the group pictured above; churches have adapted this model in various ways, depending on the ministry and needs of its members. But this should give you a general idea of what a typical adult small group looks like that practices the idea of the open chair and develops apprentice leadership throughout the life span of the group.

Carl George uses the terminology below to describe various roles in a small group. He uses this terminology so that various churches can talk about small groups using the same language. However, each church usually has their own names for the roles represented above. For example, those who would be identified as an "X" (a leader of ten) are called "small group leaders." An "L" is an overseer of up to fifty people, responsible for overseeing up to five small groups. The "L" may be called a "coach." Refer to the diagram as you study the definition of each term.

X   A small group leader of up to ten members. The Roman numeral "X" (ten) is used to describe the span of care of the average small group leader in a church. In order to honor this span of care, no leader should care for more than ten persons.

Xa   This is an apprentice leader. Apprentices learn to lead by participating in a group led by a capable leader. In addition, rising apprentices (RXa) may be present in a group.

B   This is a baby-sitter. Some groups use a baby-sitter on site to care for children.

H   The role of the hospitality person (this may vary from time to time in a group) is to provide a safe and caring environment for the small group meetings.

ECR   This stands for "Extra Care Required." Each of us, at one time or another, becomes a person who requires extra care. Whether because of family background, past history, or present crisis, the ECR person needs a special dose of love and care from God and from the group. Most groups have one or two ECR's at any given time.

G   This letter represents the growing disciples in a small group. These are Christians who are maturing in their faith.

Open Chair   The picture of the open chair represents the desire in the church to assimilate and include new people into the group structure. From time to time, groups invite and assimilate new members so that those who need and desire discipling and care can be incorporated into group life.

S   Some groups are prepared to receive seekers. In such cases, group leaders and members must be sensitive to the needs and spiritual maturity level of a seeker.

L   This is a coach. Coaches typically oversee three to five small group leaders. They are essentially responsible for a small group structure that could include as many as fifty small group members. Coaches visit groups from time to time to provide encouragement, support, problem solving, and prayer.

A Small Group Division

Small group leaders and coaches are not asked to minister on their own. We have designed a structure in which leaders and coaches can be cared for as they care for others. This structure is a "division" (or, in some churches, a "district." A given ministry area (e.g., Singles, Couples, Community Care, etc.) might have several small group divisions within it. Each division is led by a Willow Creek staff member whose job is to provide care and support to the volunteer coaches and small group leaders in their division.

As the chart below indicates, an entire structure of support has been put in place to make sure the small group leaders, or coaches, are appropriately cared for and equipped for ministry. Every small group leader has a coach to support them. Every coach has a division leader (a staff member) to support them. In larger churches, a division leader may have a ministry director or area leader to support *them*. Ideally, no coach should have more than five small groups to work with; no division leader should have more than ten coaches to care for.

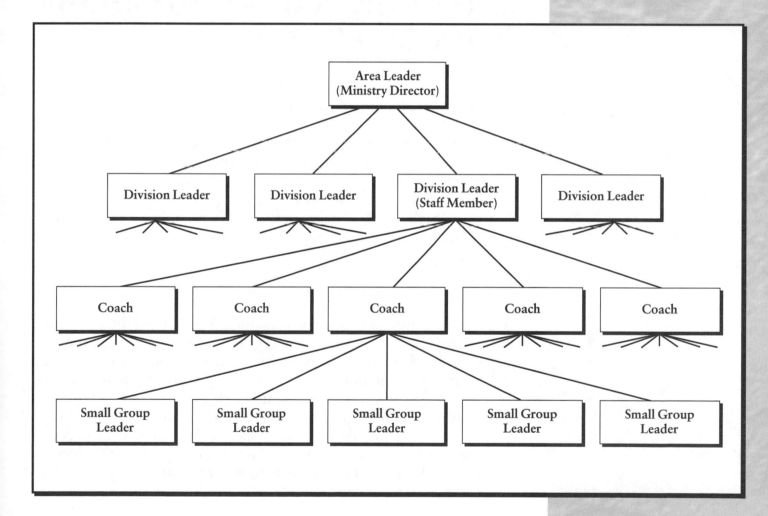

Resources

Commonly Asked Questions about Small Groups

Q *Why use this small group model?*

A This model can be used to meet many key needs in the church: to shepherd and care for the large numbers of attenders at Willow Creek, to disciple people, to assimilate newcomers and connect them to the church, to develop lay leadership and empower them for ministry, and to "be the church" by creating small communities that encourage one another in Christ.

Q *Who is the most important person in this structure?*

A The most important person in the church varies depending on your personal needs at any given time. For example, the most important person in the church might be a youth leader for your son or daughter. Or it might be a counselor for a particular personal need. Instead, we refer to the most *strategic* people in the church. The most strategic people in the church are the small group leaders and coaches who effectively carry out the mission by shepherding members and developing future leaders. They are the "front-line" agents of life change and have the greatest opportunity to affect the most people over the longest period of time.

Q *What is the primary emphasis: discipling or providing care?*

A The discipling and caregiving balance varies from ministry to ministry. However, it is our desire to emphasize each appropriately. We want to disciple people—teach them the Scriptures, help them develop spiritual disciplines, understand the Christian faith, and become disciplers of others. But we also want to care for people—to pray for them, encourage them, meet their needs for affirmation and acceptance. Thus we fulfill both the Great Commission (to make disciples of all nations, Matt. 28:18–20) and the great commandment (to love one another, John 13:34–35).

Additional Resources

▶ Books

The Power of Vision by George Barna (Regal)
> An excellent resource that contains principles for every leader who wants to develop a vision for life and ministry.

Prepare Your Church for the Future by Carl George (Revell)

Part Two

The Making of a Leader

Biblical Leadership

The Foundation of Biblical Leadership

Biblical leadership is the task of leading God's people into mutual ministry with one another for the purpose of building up the body of Christ and reaching out to the world (Eph. 4:11–13; Matt. 28:18–20). In order to accomplish this task, leaders need to

- establish a growing and maturing relationship with the Lord (John 15:5)

- sense a calling or passion from the Lord to lead people (Ex. 3:1–10; John 21:15–17)

- have a vision for building up future leaders (2 Tim. 2:2)

By far the most challenging model of leadership in the Bible is the Lord Jesus Christ. Jesus said "follow me" (Matt. 4:19), expecting men and women to abandon self-centered lifestyles and follow Him. In return, He gave meaning and purpose to their lives. He nurtured, trained, and equipped them for a mission that was far bigger than anything they could have imagined. What caused people to follow after Christ? Two things: His vision and His example.

Jesus had a compelling vision. He was looking for men and women who were willing to become His disciples and go into the world on His behalf (Matt. 28:18–20; Acts 1:8). In Matthew 9:36–38, we find Jesus casting vision for His disciples. "When he saw the crowds, he had compassion on them, because they were harassed and helpless, like sheep without a shepherd. Then he said to his disciples, 'The harvest is plentiful but the workers are few. Ask the Lord of the harvest, therefore, to send out workers into his harvest field.'" Jesus saw thousands of neglected people in cities and communities who needed shepherds. Leaders are shepherds who have a vision and a plan to appropriately care for and lead people.

But Jesus not only had a vision—He embodied the vision by becoming an example. The Scriptures provide us with the most vivid example of all when "he got up from the meal, took off his outer clothing, and wrapped a towel around his waist. After that, he poured water into a basin and began to wash his disciples' feet, drying them with the towel that was wrapped around him" (John 13:4–5). This was the explicit role of a servant of a household. Why did Jesus do this menial task? To show us that leaders lead by example. Leaders serve those they are leading; no task is "beneath" a leader. In Mark 10:45, Jesus tells His disciples that He did not come to be served but to serve. This is a true shepherd. As a small group leader, you too are a shepherd. A shepherd really cares for the flock as if they were his or her own children (1 Thess. 2:5–12).

A leader is also an example to his or her small group and should model Christ-likeness. Paul told his disciples to imitate him and to follow his example in such passages as 1 Corinthians 11:1 and Philippians 3:17. As you grow and mature in your relationship with the Lord, maintaining the simplicity and purity of devotion to Christ (2 Cor. 11:3), your group members will grow with you. Jesus tells us in Matthew 10:24–25 that a student will become like his teacher. The decisions you make, the language you use, the actions you take, your behavior, attitude, and habits, both good and bad, may be imitated in the life of those you lead (1 Thess. 1:6). This is why character and maturity before the Lord is essential to biblical leadership.

Biblical leadership flows out of a life of devotion to Christ. You impart to others what has been imparted to you. That is why biblical leadership requires both depth of character and competence. People can discern the evidence of both. Be a leader of character as you become a leader of competence. Competence will come as you develop your skills; character is a matter of your heart. In the end, God will reward those who finished well because of the depth of their character, not simply the size of their group.

Pray that you will have a heart to lead others through casting a compelling vision and by being a Christlike example.

🔑 Key objectives for a biblical leader

- Lead through serving your people well

- Multiply your ministry into the life of another

- Finish the race with integrity

Qualifications of Small Group Leadership

Leaders are servants who communicate God's truth and lead their groups in prayer, ministry, and spiritual growth. As a leader, you model the Christian life to others. In order to mature as a competent Spirit-filled leader, check yourself against the following biblical characteristics. Use these qualifications as a guide for your spiritual development, and devote yourself to prayer, reading of Scripture, fellowship, the filling of the Spirit, and servanthood so that you might develop as a leader.

▶ *Christ Follower*—Having a Passion for Christ

Our goal as believers is to become complete in Christ (Col. 1:28). Though a leader is not expected to be perfect, one is to be mature as described in Ephesians 4:13, which says, ". . . until we all reach unity in the faith and in the knowledge of the Son of God and become mature, attaining to the whole measure of the fullness of Christ." Here are some areas in which to grow in maturity:

- Turn from sin in your life (1 John 1:9; Rom. 6:6)

- Spend time in God's Word and in prayer (Col. 3:16; 1 Peter 2:2)

- Be filled with the Spirit—let the Spirit control you (Rom. 7:6; Eph. 5:18)

- Use your gifts in ministry (Rom. 12:3–8; 1 Peter 4:10–11)

- Learn to persevere in adversity (Rom. 5:3–5; Phil. 1:29; 1 Peter 4:12–14)

▶ *Character*—Paying Attention to the Heart

Depth of character is a matter of becoming more like Christ and less like the world. It also refers to the spiritual qualities or characteristics listed below:

- Being transformed into the image of Christ instead of conformed to the world (Rom. 8:28–30; 12:1–2; Phil. 1:9–10)

- Developing a character worthy of leadership (1 Thess. 1:3; 1 Tim. 1:5; 3:1–15; 6:11; Titus 1:5–9)

▶ *Calling*—Called to Shepherd God's People

Leaders have a heart for being caregivers. They see others with compassion, as Christ saw them in Matthew 9:36–38—distressed and downcast, in need of a good shepherd who will protect them and provide nurturing care for them. Deep in their hearts, leaders are convicted about the need to do ministry and use their gifts to shepherd others (Phil. 1:8; 1 Thess. 2:7–8; 1 Peter 5:1–4).

▶ *Competence*—Able to Lead and Guide a Group

Leaders set direction, keeping the group focused and guided toward its purpose. Leaders also take the time to develop the skills they need to effectively facilitate a small group (Matt. 4:19; 9:36–38; Acts 6:1–7).

► *Compatibility*—Having the Temperament and Passion for Leadership

Leaders lead well because it is part of the way the Holy Spirit has designed them. Their design is compatible with the ministry to which they are called and with people with whom they must work. Teamwork in leadership is essential. Using their spiritual gifts to lead alongside others is the kingdom design for ministry (Acts 6:2; Rom. 12:8; Heb. 13:7, 17).

► *Commitment*—Doing What it Takes

Spirit-led leaders are committed to the vision of the ministry, to Christ, to their calling, and to helping develop the members of their groups. They realize that leadership requires commitment, not convenience. Leaders are committed to seeing people grow in Christ and to reaching new people for Christ as they are able (Matt. 28:18–20; Rom. 16:3–4; 2 Tim. 2:2).

► *Capacity*—An Ability to Serve People and Provide Care for Them

Leadership is serving others and doing whatever it takes to accomplish the ministry. This means having time, energy, and resources at your disposal. Leaders must free themselves from unnecessary commitments and distractions so that they have the capacity (spiritual, emotional, and physical resources) to do what God has called them to do (1 Tim. 3:4–5, 12).

The small group leader who is committed to developing and growing in the areas listed above will faithfully fulfill the mission Christ has given His church.

Motives for Leadership

► Appropriate Motives for Leadership

Glorify the Lord

"Whatever you do, work at it with all your heart, as working for the Lord, not for men, since you know that you will receive an inheritance from the Lord as a reward. It is the Lord Christ you are serving" (Col. 3:23–24).

Bear fruit in your life

"This is to my Father's glory, that you bear much fruit, showing yourselves to be my disciples" (John 15:8).

"The spiritual leader will choose the hidden pathway of sacrificial service and the approval of His Lord rather than the flamboyant assignment and the adulation of the unspirited crowd."

J. Oswald Sanders

Keep watch (shepherd) others

"Keep watch over yourselves and all the flock of which the Holy Spirit has made you overseers. Be shepherds of the church of God, which he bought with his own blood" (Acts 20:28).

Be an example

"Be shepherds of God's flock that is under your care, serving as overseers—not because you must, but because you are willing, as God wants you to be; not greedy for money, but eager to serve; not lording it over those entrusted to you, but being examples to the flock. And when the Chief Shepherd appears, you will receive the crown of glory that will never fade away" (1 Peter 5:2–4).

Use your gifts to serve one another

"It was he who gave some to be apostles, some to be prophets, some to be evangelists, and some to be pastors and teachers, to prepare God's people for works of service, so that the body of Christ may be built up until we all reach unity in the faith and in the knowledge of the Son of God and become mature, attaining to the whole measure of the fullness of Christ" (Eph. 4:11–13).

Give God's message of reconciliation

"... that God was reconciling the world to himself in Christ, not counting men's sins against them. And he has committed to us the message of reconciliation. We are therefore Christ's ambassadors, as though God were making his appeal through us. We implore you on Christ's behalf: Be reconciled to God. God made him who had no sin to be sin for us, so that in him we might become the righteousness of God" (2 Cor. 5:19–21).

▶ Wrong Motives/Hindrances to Leadership

Self-exaltation

"Let another praise you, and not your own mouth; someone else, and not your own lips." (Prov. 27:2)

To feel important or gain prestige

"We speak as men approved by God to be entrusted with the gospel. We are not trying to please men but God, who tests our hearts. You know we never used flattery, nor did we put on a mask to cover up greed—God is our witness. We were not looking for praise from men, not from you or anyone else" (1 Thess. 2:4–6).

"I believe it might be accepted as a fairly reliable rule of thumb that the one who is ambitious to lead is disqualified as a leader."

A. W. Tozer

Because someone pressured you

"Be shepherds of God's flock that is under your care, serving as overseers—not because you must, but because you are willing, as God wants you to be" (1 Peter 5:2).

Having a short fuse or exhibiting outbursts of anger

James tells us that the anger of man does not achieve the righteousness of God (James 1:19–20). God's work is accomplished by one who listens attentively, speaks only when necessary, and is slow to anger. Leaders manage their anger or channel anger appropriately. Anger is to be put aside or properly managed (Gal. 5:20; Eph. 4:31; Col. 3:8).

Unconfessed sin

We are commanded to confess our sins. John says, "If we confess our sins, he is faithful and just and will forgive us our sins and purify us from all unrighteousness" (1 John 1:9). Any sin that has control of us (Rom. 6:16) must be confessed and brought under the lordship of Christ (Acts 2:38). If there is any outstanding sin in the life of a leader and it is not dealt with appropriately, this could disqualify a leader.

Biblical error or false teaching

Paul wrote Timothy and warned him to watch for false teachers who lead people away from the words of the faith and of sound doctrine: "For the time will come when men will not put up with sound doctrine. Instead, to suit their own desires, they will gather around them a great number of teachers to say what their itching ears want to hear. They will turn their ears away from the truth and turn aside to myths" (2 Tim. 4:3–4).

> *Leaders are called and gifted of God to build into others, facilitate their growth, and lead by example in obedience and character. The quality of ministry is directly proportional to the quality of leadership.*

Leadership Responsibilities

The Small Group Leader's Job Description

Before a person can consider becoming a leader, some prior conditions must be met. An application for small group leadership must be submitted to your division leader or ministry director. Those who want to lead a small group must be in complete agreement with the following statements:

- I confess that Jesus Christ is my Forgiver and Leader (Savior and Lord).

- I regard the Bible as the authoritative guide to my faith and life.

- I am a participating member of my church (or am actively pursuing membership).

- I agree to come into the small groups leadership structure and fulfill the requirements of a leader.

Small Group Leadership Responsibilities

You must be willing to commit to doing the following four major tasks:

▶ Build a Leadership Team

Your leadership team should consist of you, an apprentice whom you will mentor and train, and a host or hostess for your small group meeting.

How to build a leadership team

1. Sense God's calling for you to lead a small group.

   a. Do you have a passion for nurturing others in the Lord (John 21:15–17; 1 Peter 5:1–4)?

   b. Do you enjoy relating to others in a way that brings them together in group life (Heb. 10:24–25)?

   c. Do you sense you have a genuine walk with God that will be an example to others (1 Thess. 2:10–13)?

2. Choose a person to mentor as you lead your group (an apprentice).

   a. Choose someone who has the desire to demonstrate the characteristics of a small group and who desires to help others grow spiritually (2 Tim. 2:2).

   b. Include your apprentice in as many of your leadership activities as you can. Spend time with this person to disciple him or her (Matt. 4:18–22; Mark 3:13–15; 2 Tim. 3:10).

3. Find a host/hostess for your group (a place to meet and a person to be responsible for the meeting place).

   a. Work with your host/hostess to plan your meeting schedule and any other important details such as refreshments and child care if necessary.

   b. Remember to update your meeting schedule regularly with your host/hostess.

4. Receive the training needed to lead a small group and continue growing spiritually as a leader.

   a. Participate in:

      • leadership huddles with your coach for information, problem solving, support, leadership gatherings, and celebrations

      • training events as needed or as recommended by your coach

      • annual small group leadership retreat

   b. Make sure you are spending consistent time in the Word of God and in prayer (Ps. 1:1–3; Acts 1:13–14). You cannot spiritually impart what you do not have. Only growing leaders produce growing Christians. Read your Bible, asking God to teach you and give you a vision for your group.

   c. Work through this book with your caregiver (coach, division leader, or ministry director).

"And the things you have heard me say ... entrust to reliable men who will also be qualified to teach others."

Paul to Timothy—
2 Tim. 2:2

▶ Conduct Life-Changing Group Meetings

As the small group leader, your responsibility includes assembling the group and leading the time in a way that facilitates self-disclosure, understanding and application of the Word, and mutual care and support.

Leading your small group

1. Identify who will be in your group and challenge them to make a commitment for a period of time. It is best to meet with each individual (or couple) to get to know them before inviting them to be in your group. A group can grow to about eight to twelve people and still experience discussion and vulnerable sharing.

   a. Use the natural connections or relationships that you already have to find your group. This might include people in your ministry, neighborhood, place of work, or acquaintances. Remember, the body of Christ is diverse, so your group might include various kinds of people as well.

   b. Set your meeting time, place, and frequency. We recommend that you hold a group meeting at least twice a month (consider your ministry when determining this).

2. Use the most appropriate resources available for small group study that seem to fit the needs of the group.

   We recommend any biblically based material that is application-oriented and good for discussion.

3. Share the responsibility of teaching, leading discussions, social time, prayer, and ministry involvement with gifted members of your group. Don't feel as though you have to do everything for the group. Use your apprentice.

   Some in your group might be more gifted than you in certain areas. Allow them to exercise their gifts in the group, such as teaching, leading worship, leading prayer, care-giving, et cetera.

4. On a monthly basis, report the progress of your group using the Touching Base (TB) forms your coach provides.

▶ Shepherd the Members of Your Group

It is your spiritual responsibility to care for and nurture your small group members so they become fully devoted followers of Christ and participating members of the church.

Shepherding the members of your group

1. Pray for your meeting time and for each member of the group (Phil. 1:3–11; Col. 1:9–12).

2. Exercise oversight of your members (1 Peter 5:1–3). Another word for oversight is *care* or *shepherd*. It means to be concerned about the welfare of each member of your group just as you are concerned about your own welfare (Phil. 2:4, 20–21).

3. Model Christlikeness to your group. Serve them as Christ served His disciples with acts of kindness (John 13:1–5). Help them grow in Christ. Encourage one another to live each moment of life as Christ would.

4. Create a safe place for others to share their feelings, hurts, pains, and concerns. People will be only as vulnerable as you are. Admit your weaknesses to the group in a way that encourages others to see themselves as they truly are (2 Cor. 4:7; 12:10).

▶ Expand the Ministry

As the Lord grows the group, it will be necessary to consider birthing a new group in order to provide the appropriate amount of care for each person and to allow others in the church to experience life change through small groups. This should only be done when you feel the group is ready to birth and when the apprentice is appropriately trained.

Expanding the ministry

1. Use the open chair to invite others to your group. There are many people who are in relationship with your group members that are unconnected to your church.

   a. Invite prospective new members to a social event with your group.

   b. Get a feel from the group on whether these new members would be a good fit. You might need to cast the vision that growth is healthy and normal for a good group.

2. Encourage each group member to maintain a healthy relationship with the church. Members should aspire to become fully devoted followers of Christ who participate actively in the life of the body. This is best done by modeling it yourself.

3. Develop your apprentice by providing him or her with leadership responsibilities and people to shepherd. It is likely that these people will join the apprentice to form the nucleus of a new group.

⚷ Key Skills for Small Group Leaders

Here are the four main categories of skill development and growth for small group leaders. Examples of key skills are included under each category. As you can see, these areas correlate with the areas of responsibility on the job description.

Develop Leadership

- Character development
- Vision casting
- Knowing why and how to develop an apprentice
- Mentoring
- Managing group logistics
- Modeling accountability

Shepherd Members

- Caregiving
- Building relationships
- Prayer in the group
- Resolving conflict
- Meeting special needs
- Serving together
- Practice listening skills

Conduct Meetings

- Planning a meeting
- Troubleshooting
- Asking good questions
- Leading discussions
- Using the Bible in groups
- Choosing curriculum
- Opening a meeting creatively
- Praying creatively with the group
- Evaluating progress

Multiply the Ministry

- Filling the open chair
- "Fishing pond" activities
- The birthing process
- Minimizing the trauma of birthing
- Subgrouping

Personal Growth

How to Study the Bible

Most Bible study methods emphasize what the Bible says and what the Bible means. But most of the Bible, read in its context, has obvious principles to apply to life. Spend most of your time in application. Limit your study time to a reasonable passage and spend time meditating and praying about *how* to live the truth. Discuss your thoughts with others who can spur you on to love and good deeds (Heb. 10:24–25).

▶ Observations (What does the text say?)

Translation

Read the entire passage through several times. Try using several different translations (NIV, NASB, NRSV, NKJV, Living Bible, The Message, etc.) for a fresh look at each passage. This will help you identify key words and develop insights into the text.

Context

Answer the following in writing:

1. Who is writing/speaking and to whom? What is their relationship?

2. What is discussed? What is happening?

3. Where does the event/communication take place?

4. When does this take place relative to other significant events?

5. Why does the speaker say what he does? (What problems were the recipients facing?)

6. How does this passage fit into the context? (e.g., What comes before and after? How is God using this to speak to me?)

"God's Word illuminates. It penetrates our clouds of self-deception and shows things as they really are. It takes courage to step into the light in this way."

Jim Peterson
Lifestyle Discipleship

Structure

Examine the structure of the passage and make note of any significant connecting words that help you understand the author's argument (e.g., "therefore," "but," "and," etc.). Try to paraphrase the passage using your own words. Are there any key words that help you understand the author's emphasis?

Word study

List all key words of the passage and use a Bible dictionary, *Vine's Expository Dictionary, Richard's Expository Dictionary of Bible Words*, or a good study Bible like the *NIV Study Bible* to understand their meaning.

Questions

Write answers to the following as you read the passage:

1. What are the commands to obey?

2. What are the promises I can trust God to keep?

3. What do I learn about God? about Jesus? the Holy Spirit? about my fellow believers?

4. Are there any repeated words, ideas, themes?

5. Are there any comparisons/contrasts ("flesh" vs. "Spirit" in Rom. 8)?

6. Are there any lists (like fruit of the Spirit in Gal. 5:22–23)?

7. Are there any cause/effect relationships (Rom. 10:14–18)?

▶ Interpretation (What message does the text convey?)

Principles

List specific principles that you derive from your observation of the passage. Bombard the passage with questions in relation to the meaning. Proceed verse by verse, recording your understanding as you ask yourself questions like, "What does this mean? Why is it important to understand this? How did this relate to the original audience? What is the opposite of this truth? When should this be applied? How should it be applied in my life?"

Look up references to help you interpret the passage. Also, trust the Holy Spirit as your teacher. Pray, asking Him to reveal God's truth to you.

Commentaries

Consult any commentaries you can and write down insights they have that you might have missed. Call wise teachers or leaders in the church to gain their perspective. Ask people in your small group to look at the passage with you.

Theme

Write down in a sentence the main idea or point you think the author is trying to get across. You may want to write down two or three main principles you discovered that develop the theme.

▶ Application (How will I allow Scripture to transform my life?)

Teaching

Ask, "How will this truth change my life, my church, my family, my work?"

Reproof

Ask, "Where do I fall short? Why do I fall short? How can we evaluate ourselves as a group?"

Correction

Ask, "What will I do about it? What will I correct? How will others help me do this?"

Training in righteousness

Ask, "What practices, relationships, and experiences will I pursue so that I might train myself to be like Christ?

Spiritual Practices

▶ Why Are Spiritual Practices So Important?

The apostle Paul compares the Christian life to running a marathon. We run to win, reaching forward to what lies ahead, always pressing on toward the goal for the prize of the upward call of God in Christ Jesus. The runner, like the Christian, has a goal, a strategy, and a finish line (1 Cor. 9:24–27; Phil. 3:12–14). A race takes stamina, diligence, preparation, and discipline. If we were runners, we would never attempt to enter a race without proper training. In training, we learn to pursue certain practices that will enable us to endure the race.

In 1 Corinthians 9:24–27 Paul says, "Do you not know that in a race all the runners run, but only one gets the prize? Run in such a way as to get the prize. Everyone who competes in the games goes into strict training. They do it to get a crown that will not last; but we do it to get a crown that will last forever. Therefore I do

"All Scripture is God-breathed and is useful for teaching, rebuking, correcting and training in righteousness, so that the man of God may be thoroughly equipped for every good work."

2 Tim. 3:16–17

not run like a man running aimlessly; I do not fight like a man beating the air. No, I beat my body and make it my slave so that after I have preached to others, I myself will not be disqualified for the prize."

Spiritual "disciplines," or practices, will help you live the Christian life with authenticity, stamina, and perseverance. Disciplines are practiced in preparation for hearing God's voice. They prepare you for the race you were intended to run. Hebrews 5:8 say that Jesus "learned obedience from what he suffered." Practicing the disciplines prepares you to meet God and understand His will, to battle the flesh, engage in loving relationships, make wise and godly decisions, love your family, and be a leader in your area of ministry. There is great joy in being disciplined enough to finish the race. Paul wrote at the end of his life, "I have fought the good fight, I have finished the race, I have kept the faith. Now there is in store for me the crown of righteousness, which the Lord, the righteous Judge, will award to me on that day—and not only to me, but also to all who have longed for his appearing" (2 Tim. 4:7–8). Like Paul, be a leader that finishes the race well.

▶ What Are the Spiritual Disciplines?

Dallas Willard, in *The Spirit of the Disciplines*, and Richard Foster, in *Celebration of Discipline*, have compiled a list of spiritual disciplines and practices they believe were modeled in the life of Christ. These disciplines are typically organized into two categories: the disciplines of abstinence (or "letting go") and the disciplines of activity.

Disciplines of letting go

These practices allow us to relinquish something in order to gain something new. We abstain from "busy-ness" in ministry, family life, and work. We stop talking for a while to hear from God. We give up buying another material possession to experience God more fully. First Peter 2:11 warns us to "abstain from sinful desires, which war against your soul." Identify what is keeping you from experiencing greater strength and perspective. Do you talk too much? Are possessions controlling you? Are you too worried about what others think? Choose disciplines that will help you become more dependent on God.

Solitude—Spending time alone to be with God. Find a quiet place to be alone with God for a period of time. Use the Bible as a source of companionship with God. Listen to Him. Remain alone and still.

Silence—Removing noisy distractions to hear from God. Find a quiet place away from noise to hear from God. Write your thoughts and impressions as God directs your heart. Silence can occur even in the midst of noise and distraction. But you must focus your attention on your soul. This could mean talking less or talking only when necessary. And it could mean turning off the radio and the TV.

Fasting—Skipping a meal(s) to find greater nourishment from God. Choose a period of time to go without food. Drink water and, if necessary, take vitamin supplements. Feel the pain of having an empty stomach and depend on God to fill you with His grace.

Frugality—Learning to live with less money and still meet your basic needs. Before buying something new, choose to go without or pick a less expensive alternative that will serve your basic needs. Live a simple, focused life.

"… (spiritual disciplines) are meant to bring the abundance of God into our lives. It is possible, however, to turn them into another set of soul-killing laws. Law-bound disciplines breathe death."
Richard Foster
Celebration of Discipline

Chastity—Voluntarily choosing to abstain from sexual pleasures for a time (those pleasures that are deemed morally right in the bond of marriage) to find higher fulfillment in God. Decide together as a couple to set aside time to go without sexual pleasures in order to experience a deeper relationship with God in prayer.

Secrecy—Avoiding self-promotion, practice serving God without others knowing. Give in secret. Serve "behind the scenes" in a ministry that you are assured few will know about.

Sacrifice—Giving of our resources beyond what seems reasonable to remind us of our dependence on Christ. Choose to give your time or finances to the Lord beyond what you normally would.

Disciplines of activity

Dallas Willard writes, "The disciplines of abstinence must be counter-balanced and supplemented by disciplines of engagement (activity)." It's choosing to participate in activities that nurture our souls and strengthen us for the race ahead.

Study—Spending time reading the Scriptures and meditating on its meaning and importance to our lives. We are nourished by the Word because it is our source of spiritual strength. Choose a time and a place to feed from the Word of God regularly.

Worship—Offering praise and adoration to God. His praise should continually be on our lips and in our thoughts. Read psalms, hymns, or spiritual songs, or sing to the Lord daily using a praise tape. Keep praise ever before you as you think of God's mighty deeds in your life.

Service—Choosing to be a humble servant as Christ was to His disciples when He washed their feet. Consider opportunities in the church and community to serve. Learn to do acts of kindness that otherwise might be overlooked (help someone do yard work, clean a house, buy groceries, run an errand, et cetera).

Prayer—Talking to and listening to God about your relationship with Him and about the concerns of others. Find time to pray to God without the distraction of people or things. Combine your prayer time with meditation on the Scriptures in order to focus on Christ.

Fellowship—Mutual caring and ministry in the body of Christ. Meet regularly with other Christians to find ways to minister to others. Encourage one another.

Confession—Regularly confess your sins to the Lord and other trusted individuals. As often as you are aware of sin in your life, confess it to the Lord and to those you may have offended.

Submission—Humbling yourself before God and others while seeking accountability in relationships. Find faithful brothers or sisters in Christ who can lovingly hold you accountable for your actions and growth in Christ.

How to Share Your Faith

Becoming a contagious Christian

It is one of life's great thrills to clearly communicate the Gospel to a lost world so that lives can be changed and people can become disciples of Christ. To become an effective communicator of the Gospel and to understand your personal evangelism style, we recommend the *Becoming a Contagious Christian* book and training course available through Zondervan. It would even be a great idea to take your entire small group through this course!

In order to better equip you to communicate the Gospel, we have included some of the basic concepts from that course below. You might say this information serves as preparation for using the *Becoming a Contagious Christian* material. You will have the basic concept and outline to use as a way to share your faith.

▶ Effective Communication of the Gospel

Evangelism should be natural

Some people think you need the gift of evangelism to be an effective communicator of the faith. But the Scriptures are clear. Paul encouraged Timothy and the members of the church at Ephesus to "do the work of an evangelist" (2 Tim. 4:5). Once you understand your style of evangelism, you will be more effective doing the "work of an evangelist."

Your style may vary from that of someone else, but the responsibility to share our faith rests with each of us. Some people use a confrontational style, some intellectual, some relational. But whatever your style, remember to be natural and to be yourself. The *Becoming a Contagious Christian* material will help you identify your style and use it effectively.

Evangelism is relational

Begin by developing a friendship with an unbeliever. Most of us need to develop relationships with people prior to sharing the Gospel with them. Again, the *Becoming a Contagious Christian* material will provide you with ways to develop authentic relationships with unbelievers.

Evangelism must be verbal

Romans 10:14 asks the question, "How, then, can they call on the one they have not believed in? And how can they believe in the one of whom they have not heard? And how can they hear without someone preaching to them?" Ultimately, we must share Christ in a conversation where the facts of the Christian Gospel are communicated either through our personal testimony, reading of Scripture, or some other method.

Evangelism is team-oriented

All evangelism must includes the step of bringing someone to seeker events and gatherings. Churches must mobilize all of the resources at their disposal to create attractive, targeted events for seekers. You need not share your faith alone. Use the resources of your church to help people hear the Gospel in a variety of forms and presentations.

As an example of a conversation with a seeker, we focus on Jesus Christ in John 4, as He meets the Samaritan woman at the well. As you read through this passage, certain principles become obvious. Though Christ shared the Gospel in different ways with different people, this is a good, basic example of the components involved in articulating the Christian faith.

▶ Characteristics of a Christ-Centered Evangelistic Conversation: John 4

1. vv.1–8: Jesus is culturally relevant.

    a. Speak their language. In that culture, water was an important topic of discussion.

    b. Find a felt need. This woman was lonely and ashamed of her past life.

2. vv. 9–10: Jesus causes curiosity on the part of the listener.

    a. Ask good questions, listen, don't just talk, get the other person thinking and talking.

    b. In a sense, Jesus asked, "What do you think living water is?" Don't always be the one talking. Seekers are "turned off" by teachers who have all the answers; listen to them and give them an opportunity to talk about their concerns.

3. vv. 11–12: Jesus creates interest by offering solutions to peoples' deepest needs.

    The issue is the person of Jesus Christ. But people are focused on their needs (in this case, water). Jesus finds common ground in the area of need (water) and builds a bridge. Bridge-building is key to the development of any trusting relationship.

4. vv.13–15: Jesus offers to meet a person's need.

    Jesus turns the discussion toward Himself as the solution to our spiritual problem (sin). But the woman wants the solution without seeing the real problem—sin. She is still focused on her felt need.

5. vv. 16–18: Jesus' conversation leads to a personal conviction of sin.

    We lead a person to the cross. It is there they see their sin before a holy God through the convicting work of the Holy Spirit. Jesus led this woman to a point of confrontation with her sin. The sin question is often a sticking point, but if trust and openness exist, the issue can be raised.

6. vv. 19–26: Jesus desires people to become Christians, not "religious" people.

  a. They might ask, "Will I have to give up drinking?" Moral conduct follows a changed heart. This woman at the well tried to talk "religion," while Jesus focused on the relationship between God and people.

  b. Be a true worshiper of God—in spirit not in the flesh (a relationship, not a set of rules).

  c. Jesus reveals himself as the true Messiah, and the woman follows Him (4:39 ff).

For a full discussion of this passage see Lee Strobel's book *Inside the Mind of Unchurched Harry and Mary.*

►Important Verses for Evangelism

God desires a personal relationship with you

"Then Jesus declared, 'I am the bread of life. He who comes to me will never go hungry, and he who believes in me will never be thirsty'" (John 6:35).

"Whoever believes in me, as the Scripture has said, streams of living water will flow from within him" (John 7:38).

"The thief comes only to steal and kill and destroy; I have come that they may have life, and have it to the full" (John 10:10).

Sin keeps us from a personal relationship with God

"For all have sinned and fall short of the glory of God" (Rom. 3:23).

"For the wages of sin is death, but the gift of God is eternal life in Christ Jesus our Lord" (Rom. 6:23).

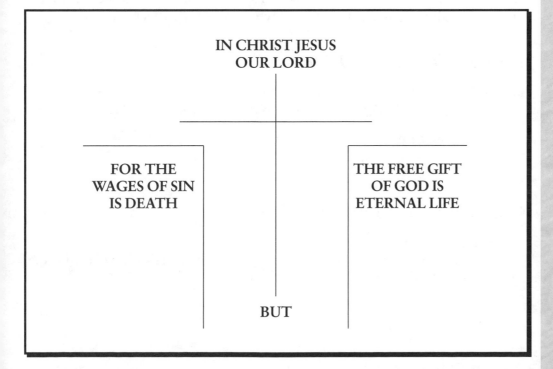

You must personally receive Jesus Christ as your Lord and Savior

"Yet to all who received him, to those who believed in his name, he gave the right to become children of God" (John 1:12).

"If you confess with your mouth, 'Jesus is Lord,' and believe in your heart that God raised him from the dead, you will be saved" (Rom. 10:9).

"For it is by grace you have been saved, through faith—and this is not from yourselves, it is the gift of God—not by works, so that no one can boast" (Eph. 2:8–9).

If you know Christ personally, you have eternal security

"And this is the testimony: God has given us eternal life, and this life is in his Son. He who has the Son has life; he who does not have the Son of God does not have life. I write these things to you who believe in the name of the Son of God so that you may know that you have eternal life" (1 John 5:11–13).

The Prayer Life of a Leader

▶ An Outline for Prayer—ACTS

You'll be hard-pressed to find a leader in the Scriptures who was effective and did not have a prayer life. All effective leaders have vital prayer lives. Here are some guidelines to help you become a more effective leader and person of prayer. We've found them to be useful and powerful principles.

We'll begin by giving you a basic outline for praying, then some principles for prayer from Romans 8, and then some prerequisites for answered prayer.

A *Adoration (Psalm 100)*

Practical Suggestions:
1. Choose one of God's attributes; list your blessings because of it.

2. Paraphrase a psalm.

3. Pray back a psalm.

C *Confession (1 John 1:9)*

Practical Suggestion:
Take an inventory of yesterday. Is there anything there that displeases the Lord? Make a list, then destroy it.

T *Thanksgiving (Luke 17:11–19; 1 Thess. 5:16–18)*

Practical Suggestion:
List your blessings using the following categories:

1. Spiritual

2. Relational

3. Material

S *Supplication (Phil. 4:6–7; 1 John 5:14–15)*

Practical Suggestion:
Categorize your needs under the following headings:

1. Major concerns

2. Relational

3. Physical/material

4. Spiritual

5. Character

Then wait and listen for the Lord.

▶ Four Principles of Prayer: Rom. 8:26–29

Romans 8:26–29 gives us some insights into prayer. As you read the passage and meditate on it, you will find some of the principles listed below. God certainly answers prayer, but not always in the way we expect. Hopefully, this information will help you understand how God responds to prayer.

1. The Holy Spirit helps us to know what and how to pray (v. 26).

2. The Holy Spirit intercedes on our behalf (v. 26).

3. God hears our hearts more than the words in prayer (v. 27).

4. Prayer is always answered (vs. 28–29), though not always according to our agenda. Bill Hybels has coached many people about God's four basic responses to our prayers.

   No—Your request is not in God's will

   > OT: 2 Sam. 12:15–16, 22–23

   > NT: Matt. 26:36–39

   Slow—Your request is not God's will at this time

   > OT: Gen. 15: 2–6; 21:2

   > NT: John 11:3, 6, 14–15, 17, 43–44

Grow—Your motives are wrong

    OT: Num. 14:26–45

    NT: James 4:3

Go—Your request, timing, and spiritual condition are okay . . . Yes!

    OT: 1 Kings 18:36–39 (cf., James 5:17–18)

    NT: Acts 12:5–7, 12–17

▶ Prerequisites for Answered Prayer

Though it is clear from Scripture that God always answers our prayers in some manner (as we mentioned above) there are also some guidelines for effective praying. Certain practices or attitudes can hinder your prayers and, in such cases, God will not respond to them. The passages below help us understand that we must be in a right relationship with God and with others in order for our prayers to be effectively heard by God.

Harboring unconfessed sin will put a barrier between you and God (Ps. 66:18).

God hears the prayers of those who obey His commands (1 John 3:22–23).

God will not hear prayers that have wrong or selfish motives (James 4:3).

We are instructed to pray according to His will, not according to ours (1 John 5:14–15).

When we pray, we are to ask in faith. Unbelief is a barrier to answered prayer (Mark 11:22–24).

An ongoing abiding life in Christ (having regular fellowship with Him) will allow your prayers to be heard. When fellowship is broken, so is communication with God (John 15:7).

Sometimes we don't have answered prayers because we do not ask. We are to pursue appropriate requests regularly and bring them to God (Luke 11:9).

Prayer in the Spirit (that is, under the control of the Holy Spirit) is also a prerequisite. This verse instructs us that we must also persevere in our praying. Prayers offered in the flesh will not be heard by God (Eph. 6:18).

If you are unable to forgive someone for something that person has done to you, then God says He will not forgive you. Restored and right relationships are essential for open communication with God (Mark 11:25).

We are to pray with thankful hearts. Those of us who come before God without a spirit of thankfulness will find our prayers are not heard (Phil. 4:6).

⚷ Key Points to Remember about Prayer

- Pray to God about everything (Phil. 4:6–7)

- Pray consistently (1 Thess. 5:17)

- Pray according to the name of Jesus—that is, the will of Jesus (John 16:24)

- Pray with bold confidence (Heb. 4:16)

Spirit-led Leadership

A common characteristic of great leaders in the Scriptures is that their lives and ministries were led by the Holy Spirit. In Ephesians 5:18–20 Paul says, "Do not get drunk on wine, which leads to debauchery. Instead, be filled with the Spirit. Speak to one another with psalms, hymns and spiritual songs among yourselves. Sing and make music in your heart to the Lord . . ." One who is intoxicated with wine lives irresponsibly before God and others. By contrast, one who is filled with the Holy Spirit leads a responsible, Christ-honoring life characterized by authentic relationships with God and others.

How can you live a life in the Spirit? Or better said, how can you be continually filled with the Holy Spirit? As a leader, you must allow the Holy Spirit to have His way in your life. This will empower your leadership and will result in your having the fruit of the Spirit.

Remember, according to Jesus in John 16:5–15, the Spirit is your helper, your guide, and your teacher for truth. Here are some ways to be sure that you are filled with the Spirit:

▶ Keep in Step with the Spirit

This is the Bible's way of saying "conduct your life in obedience to God." Keeping in step with the Spirit means allowing Him to control you as you read Scripture, pray, and hear the voice of God. By submitting your will to God's will, the Spirit can control more of your life and direct your path.

▶ Devote Yourself to the Word of God

Scripture is clear in this regard. Ephesians 5:17 says, "Therefore do not be foolish, but understand what the Lord's will is." The Spirit of God uses the Word of God to empower the people of God to do the works of God.

> "*Reduced to its simplest terms, to be filled with the Spirit means that, through voluntary surrender and in response to appropriating faith, the human personality is filled, mastered, controlled by the Holy Spirit.*"
>
> J. Oswald Sanders
> *Spiritual Leadership*

▶ Set Your Mind on the Things of the Spirit

Romans 8:6–9 tells us, "The mind of sinful man is death, but the mind controlled by the Spirit is life and peace; the sinful mind is hostile to God. It does not submit to God's law, nor can it do so. Those controlled by the sinful nature cannot please God. You, however, are controlled not by the sinful nature but by the Spirit, if the Spirit of God lives in you. And if anyone does not have the Spirit of Christ, he does not belong to Christ." Since the Spirit of God already dwells in you, you simply need to yield yourself to Him and allow Him to take control of your life. Focusing on the things of the Spirit means paying attention to God-honoring relationships, decisions, conversations, thoughts, and activities.

Galatians 5 explains that a life lived in the Spirit, with obedience to Christ's commands, will yield the fruit of the Spirit—love, joy, peace, patience, kindness, goodness, faithfulness, gentleness, self-control (vv. 22–23). However, when we are not yielded to the Spirit, we either quench the Spirit (1 Thess. 5:19) by ignoring the Word of God, or we grieve the Spirit (Eph. 4:30) by bringing resentment and anger to relationships. Sin always pours water on the fire of the Holy Spirit.

By applying the principles we've just discussed, you can live a Spirit-filled life and allow God to work through you to be an effective leader. To learn more about the work of the Spirit in the life of the leader and in the life of other believers, here are some passages you might want to read. It would be great to work through some of these as a small group to encourage others to live a life in the Spirit.

The baptism of the Holy Spirit (1 Cor. 12:13)

The indwelling ministry of the Holy Spirit (Rom. 8:11; 1 Cor. 3:16; 2 Tim. 1:14)

The filling ministry of the Holy Spirit (Acts 4:8; Acts 4:31; Eph. 5:18)

The convicting ministry of the Holy Spirit (John 16:7–11)

The regenerating ministry of the Holy Spirit (John 3:3–6; Titus 3:5–6)

The reassuring ministry of the Holy Spirit (1 Cor. 2:12–16; 1 John 4:13; 5:7)

The sanctifying ministry of the Holy Spirit (Rom. 8: 11–12; 2 Cor. 3:18; 2 Thess. 2:13)

The teaching ministry of the Holy Spirit (John 16:13; 1 Cor. 2:13)

The intercessory ministry of the Holy Spirit (Rom. 8:26)

The empowering ministry of the Holy Spirit (Luke 4:14, 18–19; Acts 1:8; Rom. 15:13, 19)

The comforting/helping ministry of the Holy Spirit (John 14:16; 16:7; Acts 9:31)

The believer's responsibility to be filled with the Holy Spirit (Gal. 5:16–26; Eph. 5:18)

Resources

Commonly Asked Questions about Leadership

Q *Do I need to have the spiritual gift of leadership to be an effective leader?*

A No. The Bible refers to most church leaders as shepherds. Shepherding gifts usually involve encouragement, exhortation, and the ability to give guidance or direction. Also, some leaders who have the gift of leadership would not be good small group leaders. Small group leadership requires certain relational skills and a certain temperament. Some leaders are gifted to have a "prophetic" type of leadership or to lead large groups of people by casting vision and proclaiming truth. Such leaders usually make average small group leaders. You should be asking yourself questions about your desire to shepherd people, your abilities to build relationships, your heart for people, and your desire to develop skills that would enable you to lead a small group of people.

Q *What is the best way to make sure I am growing and challenged as a leader?*

A Certainly, you must be regularly involved in prayer and in reading Scripture. But a leader must also have relationships in which he or she is held accountable for spiritual growth and maturity. These relationships will develop in your small group, with other leaders in your huddle, and with ministry leaders in your area of ministry. But it is your responsibility to take the initiative and step toward creating mutually encouraging relationships with people. A leader cannot expect to sit back and wait for others to come and seek relationships. Leaders must initiate them. That is part of being a leader.

Q *What if I don't currently possess the many qualities listed for competent spiritual leadership?*

A None of us possesses all of the qualities of Christian leadership in their fullest sense; each of us is growing toward Christlikeness. It is most important that you understand the areas in which you need to grow and are working with your caregiver or ministry leaders on a plan to help you grow in those areas. Remember, you'll want to grow in character and in competence—both are essential for quality leadership.

Additional Resources

 ## ▶ Books

On Leadership:

Everyone's a Coach by Don Shula and Ken Blanchard (Zondervan)
> "Whether you are a CEO of a company, a Cub Scout leader, a supervisor with four people reporting to you, or a parent, you have the potential to help others become winners in life," says co-author and seasoned motivator Ken Blanchard. He and Shula share five proven secrets anyone can use to become a great leader.

Leaders by Warren Bennis and Burt Nanus (Harper and Row)
> Bennis and Nanus focus on managing yourself and the leader, creating vision, communicating your vision, developing trust, and organizational management. It is a book that emphasizes strategies for personal and organizational leadership.

Leadership is an Art by Max DePree (Doubleday)
> DePree is a Christian in the marketplace. He was formerly CEO of Herman Miller, Inc. *Fortune* magazine said his company was one of the ten best managed in America. He brings great principles of leadership for personal growth and for application in the marketplace.

The Making of a Leader by Robert Clinton (NavPress)
> Probably the best current book on Christian leadership. Clinton emphasizes the six stages of leadership development, and he establishes checkpoints to clarify where you are in each stage of the process. Also very helpful for maturing new leaders under your care.

Spiritual Leadership by J. Oswald Sanders (Moody)
    Sanders writes that spiritual leadership is the blending of natural
        and spiritual qualities. His book is a Christian classic. Though
        a little dated, and written primarily to men, it is a thorough,
        biblically principled book on Christian leadership.

Using the Bible in Groups by Roberta Hestenes (Westminster)
    A classic on how to do group Bible study and discussion.

On Prayer:

Lord, Change Me! by Evelyn Christenson (Victor)

Prayer by Richard Foster (Harper SanFrancisco)

Power Through Prayer by E. M. Bounds (Moody)

Too Busy Not to Pray by Bill Hybels (InterVarsity)

On the Holy Spirit:

Flying Closer to the Flame by Charles Swindoll (Word)

Keep in Step with the Spirit by J. I. Packer (Revell)

On Evangelism:

Becoming a Contagious Christian by Bill Hybels and Mark Mittelberg
    (Zondervan)

How to Give Away Your Faith by Paul Little (InterVarsity)

Out of the Saltshaker by Rebecca Pippert (InterVarsity)

On Spiritual Disciplines:

Celebration of Discipline by Richard Foster (Harper SanFrancisco)

The Spirit of the Disciplines by Dallas Willard (Harper SanFrancisco)

▶Part Three

Developing
Apprentice
Leaders

Apprentice Development

Identifying Apprentice Leaders

▶ Why Do I Need an Apprentice Leader?

The vitality and effectiveness of any local church is directly related to the quality of its leadership. The meta-church small group model emphasizes the ongoing development of leaders in the body. It is the responsibility of the church to identify and develop new leaders so that the mission of the Gospel can be accomplished and so that people can be shepherded. Jesus modeled this with the twelve disciples, and Paul exhorted Timothy to do the same (2 Tim. 2:2). We at Willow Creek are firm believers in the Ephesians 4:12 concept of mobilizing and building up the body of Christ so that each member can accomplish the ministry God has given him or her. Remember, the Gospel is always one generation away from extinction. It is the duty and privilege of all small group leaders to train up a new generation of leaders and to pass the baton effectively. The future hangs in the balance. So work together as a team—leaders, coaches, division leaders, ministry directors—to continue to raise up new leaders for service in the kingdom.

> *Apprentice development utilizes the principle of multiplication. For example, an effective evangelist who reaches 1,000 people a day for Christ will win the world to Christ in 13,515 years. But a very effective discipler who teaches or trains two people a year to reach others for Christ has the potential to win the world to Christ in 33 years. As we continue to multiply ourselves, we multiply our ministry as well.*

▶ Who Finds Potential Apprentices?

Two-thirds of group leaders find their own apprentice leader. Approximately one-third are found in cooperation with a coach, division leader, and others in your area of ministry.

▶ How Do I Spot a Rising Apprentice Leader?

1. Look for group members who take the group seriously.

2. Consider those people who challenge your leadership. These may be potential leaders who are frustrated.

3. Look for gifted people whom you can recognize and affirm.

4. Pray regularly for new apprentices (Luke 6:12–16).

5. Look for people who embrace the small group vision.

6. Observe people in your ministry as they perform tasks or work with people. Give them additional ministry opportunities and responsibilities to see if perhaps they have some leadership potential.

7. Try to look for people who exhibit the following spiritual, emotional, and social qualifications:

   • Spiritual qualifications

     Do they see God working in their life?

     Are they self-feeders? (Do they consistently spend time nurturing their own spiritual growth through time in God's Word and in prayer?)

     Are they eager to learn? (Do they actively participate in spiritual discussions?)

     Do they share the vision of small groups?

   • Emotional qualifications

     Are they secure enough to be vulnerable and honest with the group?

     Are they emotionally stable? (Are they aware of their own strengths and weaknesses and not subject to mood swings that affect the group dynamic.)

     How do they respond to confrontation and character development? Defensively? Responsively?

   • Social qualifications

     Do they openly participate without dominating? (If this is an issue, how did they respond to confrontation on the issue?)

     Are they able to listen to others in a caring way?

     Are they able to facilitate discussion?

> *God's method for accomplishing His plan is people— humble, Spirit-led people.*

▶ How Do I Overcome the Objections of Potential Apprentices?

Typical objections to apprenticing include:

1. **"I just don't have the time."** Remember, people make time for those things they count as important. Share the importance of apprentice leadership in the body of Christ. Cast a vision for the life change that can occur as they rise to the occasion and accept the challenge of leading a group with you.

2. **"I don't have the gift of leadership."** Encourage people by reminding them that leadership is mostly character. It takes time to develop character and competency (skills). If you believe someone has the basic character qualities of a potential leader, remind them that you will make sure they get the appropriate training they need to be effective.

3. **"I'm not the leadership type."** At this point you need to simply explore what the person means by "leadership type." Perhaps they have a definition of leadership that is not biblical. Perhaps they view a leader as someone who is in charge and in control, as opposed to someone who can facilitate life change by caring for, shepherding, discipling, and loving others.

▶ How Do I Confirm That I Have the Right Person as a Potential Apprentice?

1. Make sure they meet your coach.

2. Have them meet with your division leader or ministry director (staff member).

3. Make sure you check with others who have ministered with this person or who know this person.

4. Confirm that they have a teachable spirit and are willing to learn.

▶ What If I Have Trouble Finding an Apprentice?

Never neglect the role of spiritual warfare in recruiting apprentice leaders. Remember, the Evil One is not pleased when we develop new leaders who can impact the body of Christ and reach the world for Christ. Prayer is essential in choosing your apprentice. Though coaches and other ministry leaders will help function as quality control managers, the role of the Holy Spirit and prayer are essential. Remember, apprentice formation is as important as the work of evangelism because this person will go on someday to create group life and ultimately reach more people.

▶ What Information Does a Potential Apprentice Need?

The basics

1. Help them understand the job description of a leader. Make sure to assure them that they are not expected to fulfill the job description requirements to the same degree as a leader would. Remember, they are a developing (apprentice) leader.

2. Give them a clear picture of the time frame for apprentice development. Apprentices require approximately 12–18 months before leading a small group on their own. However, this varies depending on the needs of a given ministry and the maturity of the apprentice.

3. Explain that adequate training and resources are available for their growth and encouragement.

4. Make sure they understand clearly the vision and values of the small group ministry. They should attend the required training events of the church. And, if they are not yet affirmed as participating members, they should do so immediately with their coach/leader.

▶ If I Become an Apprentice, What Can I Expect?

For a clearer picture of the pathway from apprentice to leader, carefully read the information below. The journey from apprentice to leader is one of the most exciting and challenging experiences in the body of Christ. In your development as an apprentice, you will need to pay attention to certain rules of the road, rights of passage, and responsibilities that are expected of you.

Rules of the road (qualifications)

Small group leadership is essentially the combination of character and skills.

Character	*Skills*
Must be developed	Can be provided
Takes time	Take practice and time
Can disqualify you from leadership	Can delay you from leadership
Involves your relationship to God/others	Involve your relationship to a task
Is an inward measure	Are an outward measure
Is tested in adversity, but developed in the quiet	Are practiced in quiet times but tested in adversity

Biblical guidelines for character and skills

Baseline Character	Baseline Skills
Mark 10:35–45 (servanthood)	1 Tim. 3:1–7 (able to teach and manage responsibilities)
John 13:34–35 (love)	Titus 1:9 (able to stand up for sound doctrine)
1 Tim. 3:1–7 (integrity)	Rom. 12:8 (lead with diligence)
Gal. 5:22–23 (fruit-bearing)	1 Peter 5:1–4 (shepherd with eagerness)

You are not expected to have developed all of these character traits by the time you become a small group leader. However, make it your aim to develop them as you mature in Christ.

Note: At this point, discuss becoming a participating member with your coach/leader.

The rites of passage (stages of apprentice development)

The three stages of apprentice development mirror the stages of early life. We've called the steps *dependence*, *independence*, and *interdependence*, and they mirror the states of infancy, adolescence, and adulthood.

1. Dependence (infancy)

   Exploring leadership

   Learning all you can

   Being an observer

   Strong reliance on the leader

   A servant's heart

   Strong dependence on the group

2. Independence (adolescence)

   You feel you can lead better than the leader can

   You think you don't need the group

   You think you don't need the leader

   You are learning the leader's role

   Warning: Though this is a normal stage in development, it is also the most dangerous, for this is the time you think you are better than your leader and that you can easily lead the group. This feeling should be an indication that you're ready to take more responsibility for the group and share more directly in the leadership of it. Your goal is not to stay in this stage of independence. In Christ, we are to become mutually dependent on one another. You must seek to move toward the third stage—interdependence.

3. Interdependence (adulthood)

You have earned the respect of the group

You respect the group

You need the group to affirm your leadership

The group needs you

You work as a team with your leader

You share ownership with your leader

You have combined the servant's heart with the leader's role

Note: Just at this time you may be preparing to birth. Don't be surprised if feelings of ambivalence, uncertainty, fear, and inadequacy arise. This is normal and healthy. As a matter of fact, these feelings will give you the kind of humility you need to become a leader. That they come is an indication to you that you are ready to birth and ready to be challenged in your spiritual growth.

The Four Responsibilities of an Apprentice Leader

1. **Love.** Love and support your leader and your group, doing all you can to be an example of the love of Christ for your people. Take an active role in loving and caring for them. Work with your leader to share the span of care.

2. **Learn.** Learn from what your leader does and from what your leader does not do. Talk with your leader and debrief each meeting, discussing the pros and cons of the process. At this point, leadership is both caught and taught. Also, take advantage of skill training as it is offered or recommended.

3. **Lead.** Ask your leader to give you experience leading the group in various ways. Begin by leading the prayer time or one or two discussion questions. Over time, work to take more ownership and leadership in the group. You become a better leader by practicing leadership skills in a "live" setting. Now is the best time to do that. You should be leading 12–18 months after you first become an apprentice. Take advantage of this time to grow and master a variety of skills.

4. **Look.** Throughout your ministry as an apprentice you ought to be looking for an apprentice as well. Ask yourself questions like:

   • Who looks like they might have leadership potential?

   • Who has a servant's heart?

   • Who is willing to learn?

   • With whom do I spend time at church that is not involved in the small group system?

Developing an Apprentice Leader

▶ As an Apprentice or Leader, I Need to Develop an Apprentice Leader—Any Tips?

1. Work through this book with your apprentice. Select various sections, and discuss how you can apply the principles and information to your group.

2. Continue to model small group leadership to your apprentice. Your example is probably the only example of small group leadership that most apprentices have ever seen.

3. Allow your apprentice to lead. Continue to delegate areas of responsibility to your apprentice.

4. Take turns with your apprentice regularly evaluating one another. When your apprentice leads a portion of the meeting, make sure you provide him or her with feedback. But also allow your apprentice to do the same for you. Create a list of questions or areas on which to evaluate one another.

5. Pray regularly with your apprentice for his or her personal needs and ministry development.

6. Help your apprentice determine what types of skill training would best fit in this stage of development. Work with your coach to direct your apprentice to the right training classes or training opportunities.

7. Bring your apprentice with you whenever you are involved in ministry. If you are going to visit someone who is sick, bring your apprentice. If you are planning to attend a huddle meeting, make sure your apprentice comes with you. Remember to involve your apprentice in meetings with your coach. When your coach visits your group, make sure the coach spends time with your apprentice.

8. Help your apprentice find a new apprentice. Remember, you can never have too many apprentices and, in order to birth, each of you will need to identify a new apprentice leader.

9. Think about using the "Apprenticeship Planner" that follows. This will help you think through how you will work with your apprentice in each month. As you can see, the planner is broken down into four main sections: (1) the apprentice's involvement in meetings, (2) their work with members, (3) personal development, and (4) long-term planning and goals. Sit down each month with your apprentice and work through a planner like this.

10. Walk them through the process of becoming a participating member of the church.

Remember, above all things . . .

"Be shepherds of God's flock that is under your care, serving as overseers— not because you must, but because you are willing, as God wants you to be; not greedy for money, but eager to serve; not lording it over those entrusted to you, but being examples to the flock" (1 Peter 5:2–3).

Apprenticeship Planner

Month	Meetings	Members	Personal Development	Long-Term Planning

Resources

Commonly Asked Questions about Apprentice Leadership

Q *What if my apprentice decides not to be an apprentice anymore?*

A This does happen from time to time. It's best to contact your coach and determine a strategy. You will probably need to find a new apprentice. Ask ministry leaders for help in identifying candidates. Remember to appropriately process the resignation of your apprentice with your group. Sometimes a member can feel shamed or inadequate because they no longer want to be an apprentice. Let them know that you support them and will encourage them to grow in Christ. Help the group understand that it is God who ultimately makes these decisions and moves in the hearts of men and women.

Q *How many apprentices should I have in a group?*

A Basically, you can have as many as you'd like. Some groups are filled entirely with apprentices. We call these "turbo groups." They usually last about six months, at which time they give birth and each apprentice goes on to lead a small group. It is best in most groups to have at least two apprentices. This allows for unforeseen circumstances (such as job transfers, apprentices who decide to step down, or apprentices that encounter great family difficulties or crises and must put their leadership development process on hold). In essence, you can never have too many rising leaders in your group.

Q *If I am an apprentice and my leader isn't giving me any leadership opportunities, what should I do?*

A First, speak directly with your leader. Be loving, but be direct. Let your leader know you are anxious to develop some leadership skills. Ask if you can lead a particular part of a meeting. Ask if you can accompany your leader on any ministry trips they take (such as a hospital visit or interview). If the leader does not respond over time, it would be helpful to contact your coach.

Q *What if the apprentice becomes a more capable leader of the group than the original leader?*

A From time to time this circumstance arises. Sometimes a leader chooses an apprentice who is actually quite gifted at being a small group leader. It is best to work this situation out with your coach, who can recommend any number of solutions, including subgrouping, birthing more quickly, or forming two new groups and seeking new apprentices for each. In any case, it's best to resolve this with your coach and ministry leaders. It just may mean that you are gifted at identifying and developing great leaders!

Additional Resources

 ## ▶Books

Biblical Foundations for Small Group Ministry by Gareth Icenogle (InterVarsity)
> Icenogle has developed a sound and inspiring theology of small groups, tracing Jesus' ministry with the twelve disciples. A great book for leaders who need a firm biblical understanding of groups and leadership development.

The Coming Church Revolution by Carl George (Revell)
> This book outlines a strategy for developing leaders in the church.

Connecting by J. Robert Clinton and Paul D. Stanley (NavPress)
> This book focuses on various kinds of mentoring relationships and how to develop them.

Part Four

Group Life

Group Formation

Casting a Vision for Your Group

A vision is inspiring. It is a picture of a preferred future—what you want to become. A vision should be compelling and something around which your group can rally. For example, a vision statement for a group might be something like this:

To become a Christlike community of faith that is growing spiritually through study of the Word, growing relationally through mutual service and caring, growing emotionally through honest and vulnerable communication, and growing numerically by adding two people to our group this year.

▶ A Vision Statement Must Be:

1. **Concise.** It takes work to get a vision statement that can be stated in a sentence or two. But this also forces a group to choose very specific words to define the vision. Long, drawn out vision statements are hard to remember and difficult to communicate.

2. **Clear.** Make sure your vision has clarity and is easily understood. For example, in the vision statement above, it is clear that the group wants to grow personally and in numbers as a group.

3. **Consistent.** Is the vision consistent with the overall mission of the church? Your vision statement for your group should somehow relate directly to the purpose of the church.

4. **Compelling.** Is your vision statement something you can sink your teeth into? Is it something worth rallying around? Does it reflect the passion of the group?

"Vision for ministry is a reflection of what God wants to accomplish through you to build His kingdom."

George Barna
The Power of Vision

5. **Easily communicated.** Can the members of your group communicate the vision? The vision should be worded in such a way that the phrases or words are easily spoken and remembered. The vision statement above is organized around the concepts of spiritual growth, interpersonal growth, emotional growth and maturity, and numerical growth.

6. **Collaborative.** Was the vision statement developed in collaboration with the group? It is key that you work with your group members (or at least the regular attenders in some ministries) to develop a vision statement that reflects the values of the group as a whole. The more that people own the vision, the more they will make a commitment to it. Remember, the Scripture says, "Without vision, the people will perish." Without a vision, the people in your group will wander aimlessly and sense a lack of purpose.

Developing Objectives for Your Group

Planning for Life Change

Date: _____

Leader: _____

We Want Our Group to Be ...

Describe a picture of what you want your group to look like in four to six months. Jot down action steps and target dates for completing those steps.

Maturing Spiritually

Specifically, in _____ months, we would like to see our group ...

_____

As a leader, I will take these steps:

By the following date: _____

Growing Relationally

Specifically, in _____ months, we would like to see our group ...

_____

As a leader, I will take these steps:

By the following date: _____

Planning for Life Change *(continued)*

We Want Our Group to Be ...   *Describe a picture of what you want your group to look like in four to six months. Jot down action steps and target dates for completing those steps.*

Fostering Safety

Specifically, in _____ months, we would like to see our group ...

_____

As a leader, I will take these steps:

By the following date: _____

Generating Excitement

Specifically, in _____ months, we would like to see our group ...

_____

As a leader, I will take these steps:

By the following date: _____

Welcoming Outsiders

Specifically, in _____ months, we would like to see our group ...

_____

As a leader, I will take these steps:

By the following date: _____

Preparing to Birth

Specifically, in _____ months, we would like to see our group ...

_____

As a leader, I will take these steps:

By the following date: _____

Components of Group Life

Though there are many different kinds of groups, all groups share some common components and values.

1. **Love.** Love is expressed in a variety of ways in group life. First, we express love to God through prayer and worship and by giving Him praise. We express love to one another as we serve one another and care for one another in our group. John 13:34–35 tells us, "A new command I give you: Love one another. As I have loved you, so you must love one another." It is Christian love that makes our groups distinctive.

2. **Learn.** Jesus said in Matthew 11:29, "Take my yoke upon you and learn from me, for I am gentle and humble in heart, and you will find rest for your souls." Learning about Christ and about His will for our lives is a key component of group life. All groups learn—they learn the Scriptures, they learn about one another, and they learn about themselves.

3. **Serve.** James says, "Faith by itself, if it is not accompanied by action, is dead" (James 2:17). Service and good works are part of any vibrant, healthy small group. Your group must decide how you will express Christian love to your community or to others in the body.

4. **Reach.** Groups must make decisions that ensure the group's purpose and vision are carried out. That means reaching others for Christ (Matt. 28: 18–20).

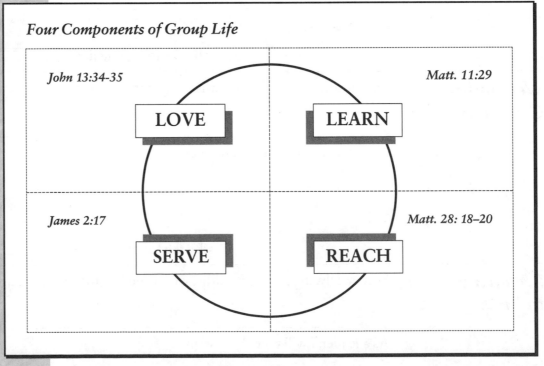

Four Components of Group Life

Each of the five major types of groups—disciplemaking groups, community groups, serving groups, seeker groups, and support groups—emphasizes these four components of group life differently. In any particular meeting (in any kind of group), one of the components of group life mentioned could be emphasized above the other. Note the diagrams which show different ways groups emphasize love, learn, reach, and serve.

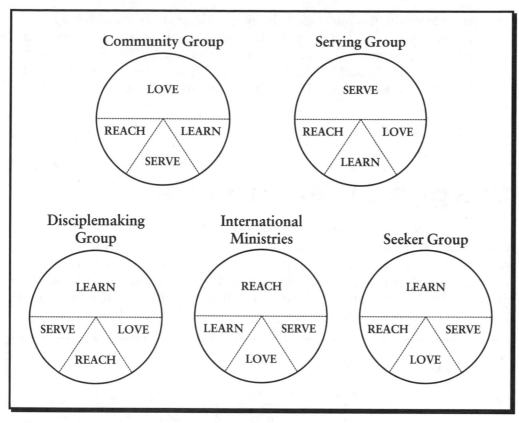

Communication in a Small Group

Communication is essential to developing healthy relationships, healthy families, and healthy churches. Communication is also essential in small groups. Without proper communication with God and with others, your group will become stagnant and superficial. The following four channels of communication (adapted from Ralph Neighbor) characterize a healthy small group.

1. **God to group.** People want to hear from God. They seek His will and desire to hear His voice. Take time in your group to be silent and to read the Scriptures. Listen as the Holy Spirit works through the Word of God to convict you and challenge you. Listen for the still, small voice of the Lord as He communicates His purpose for your group or for a particular meeting through the Spirit, through others, and through His word.

2. **Group to God.** We not only hear from God, we respond to Him. A response can take the form of a prayer, a praise, a reading of Scripture back to God, a song, or a quiet devotion that expresses feelings to God.

3. **Group member to group member.** Vulnerable, authentic, truthful communication among group members will enable your group to become a powerful vehicle for life change. Groups grow when members express feelings, words of encouragement, or hurts to one another. Remember, Jesus said, "You will know the truth, and the truth will set you free" (John 8:32). Groups characterized by truth-telling are groups that experience freedom in Christ. When members speak loving, caring truths to one another, groups avoid becoming superficial and pretentious.

4. **Group to world.** It is our responsibility as believers to take the message of Christianity to a lost and dying world. As groups, we proclaim the truth as we have opportunity to speak with unchurched people. We proclaim the truth both verbally and through our deeds. Reflect on how your group will take action to take the message of Christianity to your community and to the world.

Stages of Group Life

Groups, like all living organisms, move through stages of development. This chart will help you prepare for each stage. Often leaders take the blame for changes in group dynamics that are, in reality, simply the result of a shift in development of the group cycle. Use this chart to take a "snapshot" of your group, and to plan a strategy for moving productively through each stage. (This chart is adapted from the Small Group Leader's Handbook by InterVarsity).

Helping Group Members Process Growing Pains

Stage	Formation	Exploration	Transition	Action	Birthing	Termination
# Meetings Per Stage	4–6	6–8	4–8	10–20	4–8	2–4
Member's Questions	Who is in the group? Do I like my group?	Do I fit here? How is our group doing?	Are we really open with each other? Will this group accomplish its mission?	How will we do this? What can we accomplish together? Will we take the risk?	Will we survive? How will we change?	Did we grow? What did we learn? Will I join another group?
Member's Feelings	Excitement Anticipation Awkwardness	Comfortable Relaxed Open	Tense Anxious Impatient Doubtful	Eager Open Vulnerable Supportive	Grief Enthusiasm Loss Anticipation Fear	Respectful Reflective Thankful Sad
Member's Role	Gather information about others	Give information Accept others	Provide feedback Express frustration	Express feelings Use my gifts Take ownership Accept challenges	Express concerns Accept reality Discuss changes Give blessing	Show love Express thanks Affirm relationships
Leader's Response	Caring Clear Accepting	Affirmation Feedback Warmth Modeling	Confront Encourage Challenge	Challenge Affirm Guide Release	Listen actively Acknowledge feelings Affirm members	Review Reflect Respond
Leader's Role	Communicate vision Promote sharing Define goals	Generate trust Discuss values Facilitate relationships Create covenant	Provide self-disclosure Re-examine covenant Be flexible	Provide service opportunities Clarify goals Begin seeking 2nd apprentice Celebrate results	Cast vision Pray for birth Create sub-groups Communicate with apprentice	Celebrate Give Gifts Communion Bring closure
Content of Communication	Events Topics Facts	Topics People Group God's nature	Personal thoughts Feelings Values God's plan	Group relationships Tasks God's work	People Leadership Vision God's desires	Relationships People God's blessings
Style of Communication	Responsive General Brief	Descriptive Social Explanatory	Aggressive Argumentative Direct One-way	Speculative Cooperative Interactive Two-way Confrontive	Interactive Confrontive Expressive	Reflective Understanding Affirming

Small Group Covenants

Covenants are expressions of group values, expectations, or behaviors for which we hold ourselves mutually accountable. We enter into covenant relationships based on commitment and mutual acceptance. Covenants are based on love and loyalty, and are only valid if all parties seek to fulfill the covenant obligations. In some cases, one party may choose to keep a covenant despite the unfaithfulness of the other party (as God often did with Israel). Thus, covenants are binding agreements that can create trust and build community. Not all groups create a written covenant, but most groups have at least unwritten values or expectations that are understood by the group. If your group is the kind of group that should use a written covenant (consult your ministry leadership regarding this), then the following guidelines will help you create a covenant that serves your people well.

Keys to Forming Covenants

1. The values around which a group makes a covenant must be generated by the group, not imposed by the leader.

2. Group covenants should always be in the form of "I" and "you" statements as opposed to "we" statements. Covenants are more personal if "I" is used.

3. Covenants must be reaffirmed on a periodic basis so that members remember their commitment to one another.

4. Covenants should be created around logistics and values.

Logistics	*Values*
• where and when we will meet	• open chair
• how often we will meet	• accountability
• who is responsible for leading	• openness
• who will handle refreshments	• confidentiality
• attendance expectations	• acceptance

5. Covenants must be formed over time through a process that involves everyone. For an example of how that process might look, please look at a sample below.

▶ A Process for Making Covenants That Create Community

Meeting #1—Hand out a 3 x 5 card and ask group members to write two or three values/behaviors they expect from others in the group.

Meeting #2—The leader compiles a list of values from the last meeting and puts them all on a sheet of paper. Ask the group to break out into subgroups of two to three people and rank the values, identifying the top five.

Meeting #3—The leader presents the top values compiled from the previous week and presents a final list of the top five to seven values. (You really don't want more than five to seven. Most groups can't remember more than that, so try to focus on the key ones.)

Have each subgroup write a statement for one or two of the values, present it to the group for clarification, and then present it again in final form. This may take two or three meetings, but it will be worth it.

Meeting #4—The leader hands out the final list of values with a two- or three-sentence explanation of each. Every member signs the covenant, agreeing to operate by these values. This entire process can take two to three meetings, or you can spread it out over more meetings as the group desires.

Note: A sample covenant is shown on the next page. Feel free to copy it and use it.

Sample Small Group Covenant

1. The purpose(s) of our group is . . . *(use the back if necessary)*

2. We will meet for _____ weeks, after which we will evaluate our direction.

3. We will meet from _____ to _____, and we will strive to start and end on time.

4. We will meet at _____ (place).

5. The "serve" component of our group will have the following plans and parameters . . .(Consider going as a group one time inside the church and one time outside the church annually.)

6. The "learn" component (biblical curriculum) will be . . .

7. We will agree to the following primary values for our group:

Priority: While we are in the group, we will give the group meetings priority, and if we are unable to attend or are running late, we will call ahead.

Participation: Everyone is given the right to their own opinion, and "dumb questions" are encouraged and respected.

Confidentiality: Anything of a personal nature that is said in the meeting is never repeated outside the meeting.

Open chair: The group stays open to new people as long as they understand the ground rules. The guidelines for filling the open chair in our group will be . . .

Group birthing: After the appropriate time, this group will help start or birth other groups (after approximately 24 meetings or one year).

Apprentice leader(s): We will strive to identify and develop the apprentices in our group.

Other:

8. For the agreed time, we will seek to serve one another by sharing some or all of the following roles and responsibilities: leader, apprentice(s), subgroup leaders, host/hostess, prayer coordinator, event planner, administrator, service project coordinator, et cetera.

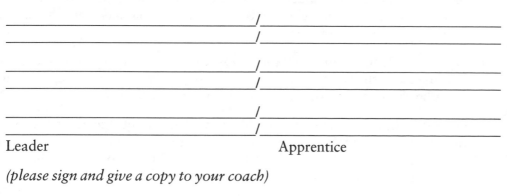

_____/_____

_____/_____

_____/_____

_____/_____

_____/_____

_____/_____

Leader   Apprentice

(please sign and give a copy to your coach)

_____

Small Group Values

"In order to see I have to be willing to be seen. If a man takes off his sunglasses I can hear him better."

Hugh Pratter

Key Small Group Values

All groups operate according to certain values and expectations. Often these go unspoken or unwritten. In order to foster open communication and clarity about the purpose and values of the group, it is important to get your core values in writing. Below you find values that are key for small group relationships. This is only a sample set of values. You and your group should create your own list with the kinds of values central to your group. Again, consider your ministry when deciding on the right approach for your group. The important thing is that your members are committed to growing in interpersonal relationships and maturity in Christ.

1. **Affirmation.** It is important to create an atmosphere where group members affirm and encourage one another, build each other up in Christ, and help each other grow.

2. **Availability.** Group members and their resources should be available to each other. People's time, attention, insight, as well as material resources, must be made available to each other in order to meet needs and serve one another.

3. **Prayer.** Prayer is valued in group life. The group comes together before God to praise, ask, confess, and thank the Lord for all He has done. Prayer encourages group members to be humble, knowing that all comes from God. In prayer, they also feel valued and come to understand their own worth. As you see God move to answer the prayer concerns of your members, the whole group will be very encouraged.

4. **Openness.** Openness in the relationships within the group promotes honesty and an ease of sharing feelings, struggles, joys, and hurts. Reaching the goal of authentic relationships begins with being open with each other.

5. **Honesty.** The desire to be honest with each other is critical to authentic relationships. In order for trust to be built among the group members, they must speaking the truth in love, so that "we will in all things grow up into him who is the Head, that is, Christ" (Eph. 4:15).

6. **Safety.** Honest, open relationships must be guarded with an agreement of safety—that what is said in the group will remain confidential, that opinions will be respected and differences will be allowed.

7. **Confidentiality.** As part of the concept of safety, confidentiality promotes openness by promising that whatever is shared within the confines of the group will not be repeated elsewhere.

8. **Sensitivity.** A commitment to sensitivity to the needs, feelings, backgrounds, and current situations of other group members will help build relationships in the group.

9. **Accountability.** In authentic relationships, accountability is voluntary submission to another group member(s) for support, encouragement, and help in a particular area of your life, giving them some responsibility for assisting you in that area.

10. **Evangelism.** As a group, evangelism is being committed to expanding the community of believers through such things as sharing your faith, using the "open chair" to invite people into the group, or other types of outreach.

11. **Multiplication.** Having your group grow and eventually birth a new group enables the group to carry out the vision of seeing more people connected in Christian community, growing in their relationship with Christ.

⚷ Key Small Group Values

Affirmation	*Confidentiality*
Availability	*Sensitivity*
Prayer	*Accountability*
Openness	*Evangelism*
Honesty	*Multiplication*
Safety	

Resources

Commonly Asked Questions about Group Life

Q *What if the values of members in our group differ from mine as the leader?*

A In order to develop a close-knit or cohesive group, people must learn to compromise. It is important for you, as a leader, not to impose your agenda upon the group. It is better to agree on a few shared values and generate trust in the group than to impose a broader set of values and offend members of the group. Certainly, there are at least two or three core values everyone can agree upon. Begin with those, and you will begin to create trust. Once trust is established, you can begin to encourage the group to consider other values as you cast the vision for the direction of the group.

Q *My group seems to bounce back and forth between different stages. Is that normal?*

A The chart that discusses the stages of group life is simply there to give you a feel for the kinds of activities and actions that take place within each stage. Actually, it is very normal for groups to move back and forth through various stages or even to cycle through the entire list of stages more than once. As groups move to deeper levels of maturity and action, they tend to repeat the stages of exploration, transition, and action. Talk with your coach to determine useful ways to work with your group through each stage.

Additional Resources

The Big Book on Small Groups by Jeffrey Arnold (InterVarsity)
    This book provides a very good basic overview of small groups.

Community That is Christian by Julie Gorman (Victor)
    This is an exhaustive and comprehensive study of small groups. It is recommended for the serious student of small group life who wants to dig further beyond the basics of small group leading and small group structure.

How to Lead Small Groups by Neil McBride (NavPress)
    Chapters 3, 4, and 5 are quite helpful for leaders who are seeking to better understand how groups form and grow through various stages of development.

Life Together by Dietrich Bonhoeffer (HarperCollins)
    A must-read for anyone who is serious about the call to Christian community.

Small Group Leaders Handbook by a small group (InterVarsity)
    This book is helpful for articulating the stages of small group life and for providing some ideas and activities for how to run your group.

Transitions by William Bridges (Addison Wesley)
    This is a secular book that addresses the issue of personal transitions and life stages. The principles discussed in the book can also be applied to organizations or groups.

Part Five

Conducting Meetings

Preparation

Meeting Preparation

As a leader, some focused, hard work on meeting preparation and planning will make your group much more effective and successful. Preparation accomplishes three things:

- Communicates to members that you have a sense of direction and leadership.

- Gives the group confidence in your overall leadership.

- Allows you to alter the course of a meeting (if necessary) because you are able to make choices regarding what issues you will cover during the meeting.

▶ Setting the Stage for an Effective Meeting

1. Carefully think through the Meeting Planner worksheet (described below).

2. Make sure everyone knows where and when the meeting takes place.

3. Identify a host or hostess for the meeting.

A host or hostess should:

- Create a warm, caring atmosphere

- Make sure refreshments, seating, et cetera, have been accounted for

- Greet people as they enter the room

►Meeting Planner and Meeting Preparation Checklist

On the following pages you will find some forms that will help you structure your next meeting. The first form is the Meeting Planner.

The Meeting Planner takes you through a process of thinking through the overall purpose of your group based on the four components of group life (love, learn, serve, reach).

Following the Meeting Planner, you will see the Meeting Preparation Checklist. It uses the acronym P.L.A.N., which stands for

- Point
- Logistics
- Activities
- Needs

Once you have used the Meeting Preparation Checklist a few times, you will be able to plan a meeting as you think through P.L.A.N. in your head. The Preparation Checklist is fairly self-explanatory. If you have further questions on how to use it or how it applies to your particular kind of group or ministry, consult your coach or ministry leaders.

Meeting Planner

Leader: _____   Meeting Date: _____

Agenda

Start	Finish	Item	Who
		_____	_____
		_____	_____
		_____	_____
		_____	_____
		_____	_____
		_____	_____
		_____	_____

Notes:

Meeting Planner *(continued)*

Leader: _____   Meeting Date: _____

Desired Outcome

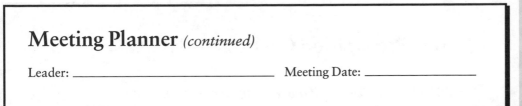

I want my group members to KNOW…

I want my group members to FEEL …

I want my group members to DO …

I want my group members to PLAN …

Post-Meeting Summary   Attendance: _____

AGENDA	PERSONAL STORIES
What worked well?	Things we celebrated:
What was weak?	Concerns:

Meeting Preparation Checklist—P.L.A.N.

P – Point *What will the meeting accomplish?*

☐ Write out KNOW, FEEL, DO, PLAN statements

☐ Write out the meeting agenda

☐ _____

☐ _____

L – Logistics *Is the setting for the meeting prepared?*

☐ Seating

☐ Distractions eliminated *(phones, noise, people)*

☐ Open chair in place

☐ Temperature

☐ Lighting

☐ Refreshments

☐ Background music during arrival

☐ Childcare arrangements

☐ Location of future meeting(s) set

☐ _____

☐ _____

A – Activities *What will happen during the meeting?*

☐ Come up with ice breaker/group mixer

☐ Special skill training

☐ Group prayer

☐ Game/social activity

☐ Gather or prepare materials

☐ Bibles, pencils, paper, etc. available

☐ Announcements to be made

☐ _____

☐ _____

N – Needs *What's happening in group members' lives?*

☐ Unresolved problems between members

☐ Financial needs

☐ Tough decision to make

☐ Health concerns

☐ Family issues

☐ _____

☐ _____

Choosing and Using the Right Curriculum

Choosing a curriculum can be an overwhelming task considering the number of options now found in bookstores. The Choosing a Curriculum flowchart was designed to help you sift through the myriad of materials to find something your group needs.

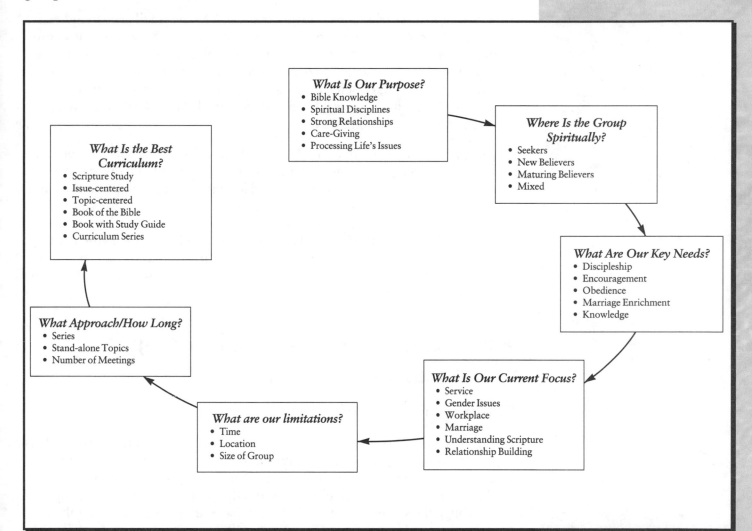

What Is Our Purpose?
- Bible Knowledge
- Spiritual Disciplines
- Strong Relationships
- Care-Giving
- Processing Life's Issues

Where Is the Group Spiritually?
- Seekers
- New Believers
- Maturing Believers
- Mixed

What Are Our Key Needs?
- Discipleship
- Encouragement
- Obedience
- Marriage Enrichment
- Knowledge

What Is Our Current Focus?
- Service
- Gender Issues
- Workplace
- Marriage
- Understanding Scripture
- Relationship Building

What are our limitations?
- Time
- Location
- Size of Group

What Approach/How Long?
- Series
- Stand-alone Topics
- Number of Meetings

What Is the Best Curriculum?
- Scripture Study
- Issue-centered
- Topic-centered
- Book of the Bible
- Book with Study Guide
- Curriculum Series

▶ A Few Tips About Curriculum

1. Curriculum should never "drive" a group. It is a mistake to forfeit opportunities for extended prayer or service, or to cut short a necessary community-building activity because "we have to get through the curriculum." Remind group leaders that Jesus did not say, "Go therefore into all the world and complete the curriculum." Your goal is ultimately to make disciples—Christ followers—who are obedient to Jesus, yielded to the Spirit, and loving toward others.

2. Never substitute a curriculum for the Bible. Curriculum and study guides should be used to enhance the group's purpose and move people into the Scriptures.

3. Don't feel obligated to finish all the questions. Competent leaders know what questions to use and how many of them to use. If a curriculum has too many questions, then choose a few good ones. I recommend five to seven questions at most. Many times, two to three good questions followed by the right kind of group process are more than enough. Better to have a great discussion grappling with a few good questions than answering all the questions at a superficial level. The goal is to actively engage people with the truth of God's Word as it relates to their own heart and growth.

4. Make sure the curriculum is "group friendly." Many small group studies are designed for understanding the Bible, not building relationships or generating a deep sense of community and caring. Look closely at not only the questions but also the process. Does the curriculum allow for lots of interaction? Does it ask personal disclosure questions that challenge people to open up and share their lives? Or is it filled with content-based "what" questions, often ignoring personal "why" questions.

An application section that simply asks, "How would this apply to your life?" is weak. But if the writer asks questions like, "It's clear from this passage we need to share our faith with others. And it is clear that we all know how and that it would please God. But let's talk about why it is so hard for you and me start spiritual conversations with seekers. Are there fears or other barriers you face in communicating the Gospel? How does it feel when you picture yourself talking to an unsaved person about Christ?" These questions will get at people's motives, thoughts, feelings, and needs. Only then can we truly encourage and pray for one another.

▶ Key Questions when Choosing a Curriculum

What is our purpose?

Each groups has a purpose, and the curriculum should support the purpose. This purpose may change as the group moves through seasons of growth, maturity, and experience. If a group starts out as a grief support group for people who have lost loved ones, the curriculum should reflect that purpose. But as people move through the stages of grieving, a leader may see that the group members need to understand more about God. As a result, a curriculum on the attributes of God may be appropriate.

Where is the group spiritually?

It is wise to take the spiritual pulse of your group to determine the level of curriculum appropriate for it. If the group is dominated by seekers, then make sure the questions are basic. Listen without making judgments, don't appear to have all the answers all the time, and deal with the issues facing them as seekers. Allow them to process information, ask hard questions, and raise objections. Use a Bible version that is easy for them to read and use. *The Journey*, a seeker Bible from Zondervan, is a great Bible for this kind of group.

New and growing believers can handle more difficult Bible discussions and are more willing to tolerate religious jargon. Even so, try to avoid using a lot of religious terminology. While believers who have been around the church longer may feel comfortable with terms like *redemption* or *justification*, avoid using them too much with newer Christ followers unless you expect to spend the time to adequately explain what those terms mean.

What are our key needs?

This question relates to the purpose question but allows a group to tie in real needs with the purpose of the group. For example, a couples group may desire growth in marriage relationships. But they may actually be in a serving group designed to help meet needs at a local homeless shelter. As couples, they could meet for thirty minutes prior to serving together for a brief study and discussion about marital issues.

What is our current focus?

Sometimes we choose a curriculum based on needs but fail to consider the long-range vision for the group. Your group may be currently completing a study on Christianity in the workplace. Now some in your group want to study Galatians. Why? How does this fit with the overall group direction for the coming year? Are there elements in Galatians that would be appropriate to focus on, or would it be better to study this book when it makes more sense in the life cycle of the group?

Try to provide a flow unless the situation absolutely dictates an abrupt change in focus. For example again, let's suppose your group is completing a personal growth curriculum like *Honest to God?,* by Bill Hybels, which has a study guide in the back. Now, it might be appropriate to identify one of the areas covered in that book and do an extended series or study on it. The section on finances and money, for instance, could be expanded to deal with using finances in a compassionate way toward the poor. This would be a great step toward casting a vision for serving others, and would not appear as an abrupt curriculum change.

What are our limitations?

Don't waste your time looking at curriculum designed for a two-hour study when your group only has 40 minutes to meet each week. Make sure you have considered the time, location (are you in a distracting environment?), and size of group (four people can deal with more questions than nine people can, assuming you want to allow everyone to participate).

What approach should you use? How long should the series go?

Should you do a long series on an issue, or should it only require just two to three weeks? If you are starting groups out of an event (like a women's retreat), then ask for no more than a six-week commitment from groups. Pick a shorter, topical curriculum (*Serendipity* Bible studies are an example). But if you have a two-year leadership development group, you can engage in a longer process. The *Walking with God* series by Judson Poling and Don Cousins is ideal for this.

Once you have chosen your curriculum, remember that it is your servant, not your slave. Use it to help people grow. Regularly evaluate and adjust your expectations. Set it aside if it gets in the way. Focus on biblical truths and life change, and you won't be disappointed.

Group Dynamics

When conducting a meeting, it's important to always be aware of the dynamics of a group. This requires paying attention to the kinds of roles people play in groups, their individual learning styles and personalities, and their spiritual gifts. The interaction of these factors makes each group unique.

Group Roles

Often members take on certain roles (sometimes consciously and sometimes without really knowing they are doing it). People will take on different roles at different stages of your group. Below are some supportive and destructive group roles you might want to be aware of.

Supportive roles

1. Information seeker—asks other members to tell more of their story.

2. Opinion seeker—takes an active interest in what others in the group think.

3. Initiator—offers new ideas, new ways of doing things. Often sets the pace in a discussion.

4. Elaborator—wants more than just the facts in a story. Adds "color" to the discussion.

5. Tension-reliever—often uses gentle humor to relieve tense situations. Uses "identification" to keep the tense person from feeling alone: "I understand. I feel that way many times myself."

6. Reviewer—tends to provide summary statements and clarity statements.

7. Consensus seeker—looks to see what the group is thinking and whether or not there is agreement on issues or decisions.

8. Encourager—finds ways to build up others in the group.

9. Standard-bearer—holds forth the values of the group and defends them.

Destructive roles

1. Aggressor—insults and criticizes others. May show strong jealousy.

2. Rabbit chaser—consistently focuses on stories or issues irrelevant to the topic at hand.

3. Recognition seeker—tends to focus primarily on his or her own achievements or successes.

4. Dominator—monopolizes group interaction. Tries to control discussions.

5. Special-interest pleader—tends to focus on personal pet peeve regardless of the topic or direction of discussion.

6. Negativist—might be a perfectionist who is never satisfied with anything. Quick to point out the "down side" of any issue or topic.

7. Quibbler—focuses on details. Often loses the forest for the sake of the trees.

8. Practical joker—rather than using humor positively, tends to distract people with jokes and comments. This is often a defense mechanism, and is used whenever a discussion gets too personal.

Your job as a leader is not to "peg" each person in order to figure out what their role is. Roles may change from time to time. You simply need to be aware that these kinds of roles exist in a group. Listen to each person with a sensitive spirit and heart. Ask probing questions that help get behind each role. If you have problems working with any one particular type of person in your group, consult your coach or ministry leaders for ways to solve the problem and deal with the relationship.

Learning Styles

Adult educators and trainers often refer to certain "learning styles." There are three major types of learning styles utilized by members of your group. An effective leader should use a variety of presentation and discussion techniques in order to communicate effectively to each learner.

▶ Visual Learners

These people respond well to charts, diagrams, and other visual stimuli. They tend to like handouts and enjoy parables and stories. They are visual thinkers; that is, they respond well to word pictures and to stories that are vivid and descriptive and allow them to "picture" what is happening.

Tips for the leader: Use handouts, newspaper articles, story boards, paper and crayons, and objects to keep the attention of your visual learners.

▶ Auditory Learners

Auditory learners enjoy learning by hearing. They would rather be in a discussion on an issue than read a book about it. Some of them may be avid readers, but in general, they would rather listen to a story than read one.

Tips for the leader: Use subgroups to allow full participation by all members in discussions. Allow members of your group to respond verbally to questions and decisions. Use background music during prayer times or at the beginning of the meeting.

▶ Kinesthetic Learners

These folks like to touch and feel things. They like to participate in the action. They learn by doing. While a visual learner might be motivated to help the poor by seeing a picture of the poor in an issue of *Newsweek,* the kinesthetic learner would be motivated by a field trip to the inner city.

Tips for the leader: Utilize objects and experiences for your group. Plan outings and events that allow people to experience truth in action. Allow kinesthetic learners to learn by trial and error, rather than by simply telling them the answer to something.

Personalities—God Made Us All Different!

The purpose of this book is not to help you identify each person's personality in some technical sense. Rather, please understand that people in your group are "wired" differently. Again, please do not spend a lot of time trying to "peg" each person in your group to a particular personality name or style. Simply be aware of the tendencies of each personality that might be in your group.

Below is a series of questions you might ask as you think of each member of your group.

1. Do they tend to be more introverted or extroverted?

   Does extensive interaction with people tend to energize them (extroverted) or drain them (introverted)?

2. Do they experience life with their senses or more intuitively?

   Do they make insightful judgments about the way life is and how it functions, or do they tend to seek experiences where they can taste, touch, feel, smell, and hear what is happening around them?

3. Do they initially process information and decisions with their head or with their heart?

   Some people are more logical and cognitive (head), while others are feelers who tend to respond more emotionally (heart).

4. Do they approach life in a structured or unstructured fashion?

   That is, are they more likely to plan out each day of a family vacation before they leave the house, or are they more likely to rent a car and decide along the way?

Group Exercise:

Why don't you give these questions to the members of your group? Ask them to identify themselves in each of these four questions. Then discuss it as a group. Not only will you have a lot of fun, but you will learn a lot about one another and learn to respect the unique way in which God has designed each of you.

Helping Members Use Their Spiritual Gifts in Your Group

Here is a process for helping people deploy their spiritual gifts in your small group. It will help the group function more effectively and allow each member to grow and mature in their area of giftedness.

1. Cast a vision for mutual ministry. Together you should read and study Ephesians 4:11–13 and 1 Corinthians 14:26. Help your group understand the value of serving together and serving one another.

2. Help members identify their gifts. Spiritual gift assessment tools like Zondervan's *Network* training course will help people identify their gifts. Go through this material as a group or ask your church to hold a *Network* seminar.

3. Discuss giftedness with each other. Ask group members to explain their gifts to the group and how they might use them to encourage other members of the group.

4. Serve in areas of giftedness. Allow people to serve according to areas of giftedness and passion within your small group.

5. Consider ministry opportunities. Discuss ministry opportunities within the group that will utilize people's giftedness.

Here are some group activities that can be shared by members of your group, depending upon their gifts and desires.

- Leading discussions
- Social time
- Prayer time
- Phone calling
- Keeping the group roster
- Maintaining a list of serving opportunities in the church
- Organizing group outreach
- Hosting the group
- Becoming an apprentice
- Leading worship
- Writing notes and cards
- Visiting members who have needs or who are ill
- Preparing for group meetings
- Maintaining calendars and schedules
- Keeping a list of birthdays of members
- Keeping a list of members' children's birthdays
- Choosing curriculum
- Providing feedback and evaluation

This is just a partial list, but it should help you and your group share the responsibilities of group life together.

▶ The Role of the Holy Spirit in Group Dynamics

We have already seen how the Holy Spirit has gifted each member of the group so that the group functions as a body. However, He also works in other ways. He guides people and teaches them from the Word. He also can work through promptings and experiences. As a group leader, be sensitive to the working of the Holy Spirit as He moves among group members. Here are a few suggestions that will help you be open and sensitive to His leading.

1. Pray that the Holy Spirit would do His work of conviction and teaching during your group meeting.

2. As a leader, be sensitive to group consensus. If the group senses there should be a change in direction, this may be the voice of the Spirit. Do not automatically assume your agenda is the right agenda.

3. If you sense a strong conviction from the Spirit of God to discuss a certain matter or issue, feel free as the leader to tell this to the group. Do not use it in such a way as to force the group to agree with you. Rather, simply explain that you sense God wants you to share some feelings or issues. Then allow the group and the Word of God to be your guide as to how you might move forward.

4. Allow time for the Holy Spirit to work. Sometimes it is best to wait if there is not consensus on an issue. Ask members to pray consistently throughout those weeks and to seek the will of God. Allow the Spirit of God to work within people over time.

Remember, the Holy Spirit wants to edify and unite a group. That does not mean all members will agree on all issues. However, it does mean that members of the group should be willing to submit to one another as they seek consensus, understanding that this consensus is likely the result of the Spirit of God working among them to develop community and mutuality. In all cases, verify or compare promptings of the Spirit through the clear teaching of the Bible. Where the Word of God is clear, obey. Where the Scriptures are silent, seek the will of God and the group consensus as each person submits his or her agenda to Christ and is willing to compromise for the sake of the group.

"While they were worshiping the Lord and fasting, the Holy Spirit said, 'Set apart for me Barnabas and Saul for the work to which I have called them.' So after they had fasted and prayed, they placed their hands on them and sent them off."

Acts 13:2–3

Skills

Group Openers and Share Questions

Using group openers is a basic, yet essential, small group skill. Icebreaker ideas and share questions are designed to facilitate discussion about members' personal lives and to help them open up more freely. They are not designed for simple yes and no answers.

Use discretion with these questions and statements. Some will evoke deep and serious responses. Others are light and funny. If your group is new, you should probably use questions and icebreakers that focus on information about people's lives (where they grew up, where they went to school, how they came to your church, where they work, what they think about certain events in our culture, et cetera). As intimacy develops in a group, begin to challenge people with more in-depth questions that evoke feelings, thoughts, and insights.

What is your favorite movie and why?

If money were no problem, and you could choose one place in the world to travel for a week, where would that place be and why?

Write down your two most favorite summer activities. Pair off and share those activities with one another, explaining why they are your favorites.

Who is your number one advisor in life and why?

One of my biggest pet peeves is _____.

People might be surprised to find out that I _____.

You have three wishes. What would you wish for?

If you suddenly lost your eyesight, what would be the thing you missed seeing the most?

What is the most daring thing you have ever done? What made it so daring?

My favorite way to waste time is _____.

You have one minute to speak to the entire nation on national television. What one or two key things would you like to tell them?

What's the story behind the longest time you've gone without sleep?

What were the circumstances that surrounded your first kiss?

Who is the most famous person you've known or met? How did it happen?

When I dated, I was considered _____ because _____.

If you could do one miracle (other than make the whole world Christian), what would you do? Why?

What do you miss most about childhood?

What's the biggest lie you ever told?

If given a choice, how would you choose to die? How do you *not* want to die?

What is your biggest fear about death?

If you could go to college (again), what would you study?

What's the worst storm or disaster you've been in? What was it like?

Decribe the most boring day/event/period of time you can remember.

What day of your life would you most like to relive? Why?

What's the smallest space you've lived in? What was it like?

I was (or would have been) voted "most likely to" _____ in high school?

Just for the fun/thrill of it, before I die I'd like to _____.

My number-two career choice would be _____.

As a time traveler, I would most like to visit _____ because _____.

What has been one of the greatest adventures you have ever been on?

If I could invent a gadget to make my life easier, I'd invent something that would _____ because _____.

Next year looks better to me because _____.

Next year may be a problem because _____.

I am most like my mom in that I _____.

I am most like my dad in that I _____.

I wish before I got married someone had told me _____.

I have never quite gotten the hang of _____.

I'm a bundle of nerves/all thumbs when it comes to _____.

I will probably never _____, but it would still be fun if I could.

What are a couple of things you remember about your grandparents?

What does your name mean? Why were you named that?

What is one of the most memorable dreams you have ever had?

If you were going to leave the world one piece of advice before you died, what would you say?

If you were to describe yourself as a flavor, what would your flavor be?

What was the best gift you ever received as a child?

If you could raise one person from the dead, who would you raise and why?

Who was one of the most interesting persons you or your family ever entertained?

What is the nicest thing anybody ever said about you?

What one thing would you like your obituary to say about you? Why?

What is your favorite city? Why?

Where do you go or what do you do when life gets too heavy for you? Why?

Which do you value most—sight or speech? Why?

When you were growing up, who was the neighborhood bully? What made that person so frightening?

What is your fondest memory of a picnic? Why was it so special?

What is the best news you have heard this week? The worst news?

What was one of the worst things your brother or sister did to you as a child?

If your house were on fire, what three items (not people) would you try to save?

What was your first job? What do you remember most about it?

Who was the best boss you ever had? What made him or her so good?

When you were a child, what did you want to be when you grew up? What did your parents want you to be?

If you could choose one different way to do your wedding (parachuting while reciting your wedding vows, holding the service underwater, et cetera) what would you choose?

Who was your hero when you were growing up? How did you try to imitate him or her?

If you could go on national television and warn your countrymen to avoid three things, what would you say?

What was your worst boss like?

I suspect that behind my back people say I'm _____ because _____.

Tell the group briefly the story of your wedding day. (If you warn them in advance, each couple can bring their pictures to share with the group.)

Tell the group what's been happening in your life lately using the following categories: something old, something new, something happy, something blue.

Why do you sin? (No simplistic answers allowed!)

In what area of your life would you like to have greater peace? Why?

If you could someday have a worldwide reputation for something, in what area would you like that to be? Why?

What is one of your biggest fears about the future?

Using a fruit or vegetable as a metaphor, how would you describe your life this week (dried fig, ripe cantaloupe, smashed banana, et cetera)?

What do you like best about children? Why?

Of the things money can buy, what do you long for the most?

If you had to go to prison for a year, what do you imagine would be the hardest part of that experience? Why that?

Describe a grade school teacher that made a big impression on you (for good or ill).

You have been granted one hour with the president of the United States. What would you ask him? What would you tell him?

You have been given a year sabbatical from work. You can't go more than 150 miles for any one period of time. What would you do?

Break your life into three equal segments. What was the most significant event from each of these periods of time?

Have each person in the group answer for every other member of the group: "I am so glad God made you _____ because that aspect of who you are is _____."

Something I have from my childhood I'll probably never give up is _____ because _____.

The most useless thing in my/our house is _____ but it's still there because _____.

The thing in my wallet/purse that tells the most about who I think I really am is _____ because _____.

When you were a child, what was your favorite time of day? Day of the week? Time of the year? Why were these favorites?

In general, people worry too much about _____.

I want to be taken more seriously in the following area: _____.

An emotion I often feel but don't usually express is _____.

Facilitating Dynamic Discussion

▶Four Facilitator Actions

A leader ACTS to facilitate discussions by

- Acknowledging everyone who speaks during a discussion

  Even if several people speak at once, make sure to recognize each one. Also, respond to laughter or a groan or a deep sigh—remember, 90 percent of communication is nonverbal.

- Clarifying what is being said and felt

  Say, "Let me see if I understand what you are saying."

- Taking it to the group as a means of generating discussion

  Don't be the answer person. Ask, "What do others of you think about what was just said?"

- Summarizing what has been said

  Offer statements like, "So far it seems like we have been saying . . ." or "Nancy, could you try to summarize the key components of the discussion so far?"

▶Questions

Another key to facilitating dynamic discussions is generating the right kinds of questions and offering appropriate responses. Here are some guidelines for the kinds of questions and responses that would help your group engage in meaningful, challenging discussions.

Opening Questions

Use an opening question to help the group warm up to each other, get to know one another better, and to let them hear their own voices. Opening questions are speculative and thought-engaging.

Broach the topic of discussion with a short, creative illustration or story that will answer the question, "Why do I want to discuss this topic tonight?"

Examples:

"What do you look forward to as you grow older?"

"What is it that often drives us to fear intimacy with one another? What can we do as a group to diminish this anxiety?"

Launching questions

Knowing the goal of the discussion, the group leader prepares launching questions designed to generate group interaction and feedback. These questions are typically designed to answer the question, "What do I know, what do I feel, what should I do?"

Examples:

"What do we learn from seeing the obstacles Joseph faced and how we overcome them?"

"After hearing tonight's discussion, we all agree that we are somewhat 'stuck.' What steps can we take to develop greater trust levels with each other?"

"What do you think was going through Peter's mind at this time?"

Some questions do not necessarily launch a discussion, but they do solicit responses and feedback. There are two kinds launching questions: those that are leading and those that are limiting.

Leading questions usually produce a short answer.

Examples:

"Would you be tempted in this situation?"

"Do you agree or disagree with this statement?"

Limiting questions indicate that you have a specific answer in mind. They do not promote much discovery. However, they can help clarify facts.

Examples:

"What three commands do we find in this passage?"

"What two things does Paul say we must do?"

Guiding questions

Even the most well-prepared leader will need to spontaneously guide discussion at times.

Examples:

Rephrase the question: "You seem to be asking, 'How can we develop trust as a group?'"

Personalize the question: "How would you respond to Jesus if He asked you that question?"

Test for consensus or decision: "Are we saying that everyone must obey this command?"

Summarizing questions

Summarizing after a series of questions allows the leader to acknowledge group members' contributions while maintaining biblical integrity and direction.

Examples:

An affirming comment can be made with good eye contact and a smile by saying, "Thanks for sharing that" or "That's a good point" or "Okay, that is a response worth considering; are there other thoughts as well?"

A summarizing response might be, "So what we see in this passage is . . ."

Application questions

The goal of the small group study is not just information but transformation. The leader can help members apply what they have learned by asking application questions.

Examples:

"What changes will you make this week as a result of our discussion tonight?"

"What difference does this make to you and me?"

▶ Responses

How you and other members of the group respond to questions or statements will either foster or fizzle discussion. Here are some tips on how to respond appropriately to questions or comments made by group members.

Affirming responses

These responses acknowledge each person's value. They promote intimacy and openness. Such responses send a strong signal to group members, telling them they have been heard, understood, and respected.

Examples:

"I understand this sharing is painful for you. I am feeling very sad for the way you were treated by your boss this week."

"Bob, I realize you want to talk, but it is important that we listen to what Steven has shared, and attempt to come alongside him during this critical time of decision for him."

Participatory responses

These responses invite others to join in the discussion. They not only affirm a participant's sharing, but also invite others to engage in the process. Participatory responses do not isolate group members by shaming, embarrassing, or lecturing them.

Examples:

"How have others in the group dealt with grief you have experienced?"

"Sam, that was a terrific insight; could you share how you came to that realization?"

"Bob has shared some deep feelings tonight. How might others of you have responded to a similar confrontation at work?"

Paraphrasing or "going deeper" responses

Paraphrasing allows you to repeat the thoughts of others and enables them to share more deeply. It summarizes what has been heard and allows the group to explore personal feelings, thoughts, and actions.

Examples:

"June, if I heard you correctly, I believe you stated something similar to what Keri shared last week. Do you share the same feelings as Keri on this matter?"

"That was a very painful episode in your childhood, wasn't it, Greg? How did you deal with it? How do you face it today?"

"It is exciting to be part of a victory like you shared, Sharon. How does that impact your relationship with your husband, Scott?"

These kinds of responses—affirming, participatory, and paraphrasing—will enable you to value your members while encouraging them to express feelings, thoughts, and personal concerns.

▶ The Dynamics of Effective Listening

Active listening involves not only what you hear, but also what you say. This means actively engaging with the person who is speaking, setting aside your personal agenda, and keeping yourself from distracting thoughts (particularly thinking about what you are going to say next!). Here are some tips for active listening.

What you say

1. Invite comments from the group
2. Empathize with people's emotions
3. Explore their statements, seeking more information
4. Clarify what has been said

What you hear

1. *Verbal:* the content of what is said. Sometimes we are so interested in what we are about to say that we fail to hear the simple facts in a discussion. As you listen, focus on people's names, events, dates, and other specific information that is being shared.

2. *Nonverbal:* how the content is expressed. Here you are listening for congruity; that is, do the nonverbal messages match the verbal messages? Listen for this in three areas:

- **Facial expressions.** When someone says "I'm okay," does their facial expression actually communicate "I'm a little sad"?

- **Tone of voice.** Listen for tones of sarcasm, anger, sadness, enthusiasm, hesitancy, fear, et cetera.

- **Body movements and posture.** Are arms and legs crossed and closed? Are people fidgety or relaxed? Does their posture indicate interest or boredom? Remember, you can "hear" a lot just by watching people's actions.

Here are some differences between active and passive listening. As a leader, how would you rate yourself?

Listening Skills
Passive vs. Active Listening

	Passive Listening	*Active Listening*
Attitude	Rejecting, critical *"I'm really not interested."*	Receptive, accepting *"I really want to hear."*
Focus	Me—what I want to say *"What do I think?"*	Other person—you think about what others are saying *"What does he mean?"*
Response	This is what I've been thinking *"I think you should …"*	Telling first what you have heard the other person say *"You think …" "You feel …"*
Message	What you said isn't important *"I didn't really hear what you said."*	You heard both the feeling and the need in the message *"I heard what you said."*
Results	Frustration, anger *"I don't care."*	Satisfaction, willing to compromise or tell more *"I care about what you said."*

This would be great material to review with your group, especially if it is just starting.

Group Prayer

▶ What Can I Do as a Leader to Help Facilitate Meaningful Prayer in my Group?

Model it

1. Be a person of prayer yourself—pray for your members, the open chair, ask God to give you His direction in leading the group.

2. When you do pray out loud in the group, keep your prayers honest, authentic, and from your heart.

3. Simple guide for group prayer:

   - Short

   - Simple

   - Spirit-led

   - Silence is okay

Keep it Safe

1. Don't call on someone to pray unless you've asked permission beforehand (or you know them well).

2. Don't expect everyone to pray every time.

3. Try to avoid praying in a circle. Allow members to pray one at a time as they feel led.

4. Respect the intimacy level. As the group grows in deepening relationships, a sense of safety will foster more genuine prayer.

Guide the prayer

1. Give general guidelines, but let the Holy Spirit lead.

2. Avoid lengthy discussions on prayer.

3. Include prayer each time you meet.

4. Use a variety of praying methods.

▶ What Happens When Groups Commit to Pray for One Another?

- Your relationship with Him and each other will deepen. You will experience spiritual growth in Christ.

- There is less chance of burnout as you put problems in His hands and trust members to His care.

- You allow the Holy Spirit to work in your group so your time together is filling and refreshing.

- He will answer your prayers in amazing ways, and your faith will increase.

▶ Creative Ideas for Group Prayer

1. Pray through a psalm out loud together.

2. In a couples group, have spouses pray for each other.

3. Vary prayer time between the beginning, middle, and closing of the meeting.

4. Pick a portion of Scripture to pray for one another during the week (Col. 1:9; Eph. 3:14–19, et cetera).

5. Pray through your church's prayer requests given in the bulletin or program each week.

6. If someone is in crisis, stop and pray for them right then.

7. Pray for the church, a country, a family in need, specific seeker-oriented events, or any area for which your group has a passion.

8. Do a study on prayer. Highly recommended: *Praying from God's Heart* by Lee Braise, or *Prayer* by Richard Foster, or *Too Busy Not to Pray* by Bill Hybels.

9. Is there someone in your group with the gift of faith or encouragement? Ask that person to be the prayer coordinator who writes down requests each meeting and keeps track of answers. If a group member has an emergency, they can call the prayer coordinator, who will notify all the other members to pray for them.

10. Praise is a part of intercession. Is a member in the midst of struggle? Praise God instead of praying requests.

11. Have each member write down requests for the week on a piece of paper. Fold the piece of paper and put it in a hat. Pass the hat, each member agreeing to pray for the person they pick and to call to encourage them during the week.

12. To cut down on the time your group spends talking about prayer requests, give everyone a 3 x 5 card to write down prayer requests for the week and have them exchange cards with another member of the group.

13. We need to get our requests from God. The next time you are asked to pray for an event, for someone's salvation or health, stop and ask the Lord, "What are Your desires, and what can I pray that will cause Your desires to take place?"

▶ What to Pray for Others: Colossians 1:9–14

Intercessory prayer can be defined as asking God to act on behalf of someone else. Sometimes we don't know how to pray for our friends and family (or even those who have hurt us), yet we know we should. Paul gave us a pattern of prayer in Colossians 1:9–14 to follow when we pray for others. Read this passage and try using it as a pattern the next time you pray. Watch how God answers.

Pray that

1. they will understand God's will
2. they gain spiritual wisdom
3. they live a life pleasing and honoring to God
4. they do kind things for others
5. they know God better and better
6. they are filled with God's strength
7. they endure in patience
8. they stay full of Christ's joy
9. they always be thankful
10. they recall God's forgiveness of their sins

▶ Biblical Examples and Styles of Prayer

The Lord's Prayer, which serves as a basic model for us (because it includes several kinds of petitions), and some prayers from Scripture give a wealth of methods, or styles, for moving your group to deeper levels of praying.

▶ Kinds of Prayer

Opening	"Hear our prayer . . ." (Neh. 1:11; Ps. 5:1–3)
Adoration	"Hallowed be your name . . ." (Deut. 10:21; 1 Chron. 29:10–13; Ps. 34:8–9)
Affirmation	"Your will be done . . ." (Ps. 27:1; Isa. 26:3; Rom. 8:38–39)
Group Needs	"Give us this day . . ." (Ps. 7:1; Neh. 1:11; Matt. 7:7–8)

"For this reason, since the day we heard about you, we have not stopped praying for you and asking God to fill you with the knowledge of his will through all spiritual wisdom and understanding. And we pray this in order that you may live a life worthy of the Lord and may please him in every way: bearing fruit in every good work, growing in the knowledge of God, being strengthened with all power according to his glorious might so that you may have great endurance and patience, and joyfully giving thanks to the Father, who has qualified you to share in the inheritance of the saints in the kingdom of light. For he has rescued us from the dominion of darkness and brought us into the kingdom of the Son he loves, in whom we have redemption, the forgiveness of sins."

Colossians 1:9–14

Confession	"Forgive us our debts ..." (Ps. 51; Matt. 18:21–22; 1 John 1:9)
Renewal (protection)	"Lead us not into temptation ..." (Ps. 137:7; John 15:7–11)
Thanksgiving	"Give thanks to the Lord ..." (1 Chron. 16:34; Ps. 75:1; Rev. 11:17)
Blessing	"The Lord bless you and keep ..." (Num. 6:22–27; Ps. 1:1)
Commissioning	"Go therefore and make disciples ..." (Matt. 28:18–20; Acts 1:8)
Healing	"The prayer of faith will make well ..." (James 5:13–16; Ps. 6:2; 41:4)
Warfare	"Get thee behind me, Satan ..." (Matt. 4:10; 16:23)
Benediction/Closing	"May the grace of the Lord ..." (2 Cor. 13:14; Eph. 3:20–21)

Conflict Management

As relationships in groups deepen, conflict is inevitable. A group that experiences no conflict among members is probably either a brand-new group or a group that has not pursued authentic relationships. Let's look at some biblical principles for conflict management and then at some effective conflict management strategies for small group leaders.

▶ Biblical Principles for Conflict Management

The distinction between quarreling and constructive conflict

Quarreling	Constructive Conflict
seeks win/lose	leads to win/win
tends to divide/choose sides	seeks reconciliation/choose steps
speaks exaggerations from strife	speaks truth in love
is an end in itself	is a means to an end
tears down	clears path toward something better
usually has a hidden agenda	is only about what is in the open
comes from a person pushing an issue	brought about by necessity in community
is a battle	is work
is usually hard	is usually hard

The Bible differentiates between quarreling and constructive conflict. Quarreling is negative because it refers to vain arguments or disagreements for the purpose of promoting self-worth or causing division. James 4:1–3 asks us, "What causes fights and quarrels among you? Don't they come from your desires that battle within you? You want something but don't get it. You kill and covet, but you cannot have what you want. You quarrel and fight. You do not have, because you do not ask God." This kind of quarreling is not pleasing to God. Paul told Timothy the same thing in 2 Timothy 2:24, which says, "The Lord's servant must not quarrel."

However, there is much admonition in Scripture for leaders to use constructive criticism and exhortation in order to bring about spiritual growth. In 2 Timothy 3:16 this is referred to as "rebuking," and in other places as "admonition" or "exhortation."

🔑 Key Scriptures for Conflict Management

Speak truth in love (Eph. 4:15, 25)

Mirror rather than try to change people's feelings (Rom. 12:15; 1 Cor. 12:26)

Seek to edify and be gracious (Eph. 4:29–32)

Express real emotions, but do not sin (Eph. 4:26–27)

Settle private disputes privately (Matt. 18:15–17)

Do not keep a record of wrongs (1 Cor. 13:5)

Think before you speak (Prov. 15:23, 28)

Do not return insult for insult (1 Peter 3:8–9)

Check your motives for conflict (James 4:1–2; Prov. 13:10)

Pursue peace and edification in relationships (Rom. 14:19)

Avoid needless quarrels (Prov. 20:3; 2 Tim. 2:24)

Remember group members' interests as well as your own (Phil. 2:4)

▶ Strategies for Managing Conflict

There are several approaches to conflict management, each having its own benefits. In small groups, however, the strategies of compromise and collaboration are probably the most effective.

Avoidance (the turtle)

Avoidance is an effective strategy to use with conflict when

- the issue is trivial

- the situation will take care of itself

- saving face (yours or someone else's) is important

- time is limited

Avoidance is not an effective strategy to use with conflict when

- the problem is important

- the problem will not resolve itself (and may worsen if neglected)

- credibility would be lost by avoidance

- there is a larger, underlying issue that is important to address

Competition (the shark)

Competition would be an effective strategy to use when

- a competitive interaction would result in a better solution

- you want one person/position to prevail over another but you cannot declare your sympathies publicly

- the issue outweighs the relationship

- encouraging competition will clarify the issue and expose weak spots

Competition is not an effective strategy to use when

- long-term relationships are important

- conflict is likely to become personal rather than remaining issue-oriented

- it is important to avoid a win-lose situation or public defeat

Accommodation (the teddy bear)

Accommodation is an effective strategy to use with conflict when

- the relationship is more important than the task

- the issue is trivial

- small concessions will reap further gains (i.e., choose your battles)

Accommodation is not an effective strategy to use with conflict when

- your actions could be interpreted as being condescending

- its use would set an unwise precedent (e.g., fee bargaining)

Compromise (the fox)

Compromise is an effective strategy to use when

- there is no simple solution

- both parties have strong interest in very different facets of the problem

- there is not enough time for a truly collaborative solution

- the situation is not critical and an adequate solution is good enough

"Life without confrontation is directionless, aimless, passive. When unchallenged, human beings tend to drift, to wander or to stagnate. Confrontation is a gift."
David Augsburger

Compromise is not an effective strategy to use when

- a dangerous precedent would be set by failure to hold one's ground

- an optimal resolution is possible

- it is important to avoid concessions of any kind

Collaboration (the owl)

Collaboration is an effective strategy to use when

- the task and the relationship are both very important

- the time, information, and willingness to collaborate are present

- the outcome is exceedingly important

- sufficient trust exists between the parties

Collaboration is not an effective strategy to use when

- time, trust, and resources are not available

- the issue is not worthy of the investment of time, energy, and resources

▶ Care-fronting: The Creative Way Through Conflict

In his book *Caring Enough to Confront,* David Augsburger describes an approach to conflict management called "care-fronting." Below is a synopsis of that strategy.

Incorrect thinking about caring: "Caring" is a good word when confronting is absent

There is a time for caring, and a person should care when care is called for. But caring dare not be contradicted by any mixture of confrontation. To care genuinely, candor and confrontation must be forgotten, at least for the moment. When someone cares deeply about another, they cannot confront, because hurting that person is the very last thing they want to do.

Incorrect thinking about confronting: "Confronting" is a bad word when compared to caring

There is a time for confronting, and a person should confront when confrontation is required. But confronting must not be contaminated by any admixture of caring. To confront powerfully, care must be laid aside. When someone is angry, they should confront. To talk of caring at a moment like that would be false.

Correct thinking about caring and confronting: "Care-fronting"

Together, the words *care* and *confronting* provide the balance of love and power that lead to effective human relationships. Unfortunately, the more common practice is to keep these distinct and separate.

Care-fronting offers genuine caring that bids another grow. To care is to welcome, invite, and support growth in another. It offers real confrontation that calls out new insight and understanding. To confront effectively is to offer the maximum of useful information with the minimum of threat.

Care-fronting unites love and power and unifies concern for relationship with concern for goals. This way, one can have something to stand for *(goals)* as well as someone to stand with *(relationship)* without sacrificing one for the other, or collapsing one into another. Thus one can love powerfully—and be powerfully loving. These are not contradictory; they are complementary.

▶ Expressing Anger in Groups

There are two ways of expressing anger in groups. "I" messages are clear and confessional. The person using "I" messages owns their anger, responsibility, or demands without placing blame. "You" messages are most often attacks, criticisms, labels, devaluation of the other person, or ways of fixing blame.

When angry, attempt to give clear, simple "I" messages.

Following are some examples of "I" and "You" messages.

"I" Messages	*"You" Messages*
I am angry.	You make me angry.
I feel rejected.	You're judging and rejecting me.
I don't like the wall between us.	You're building a wall between us.
I don't like blaming or being blamed.	You're blaming everything on me.
I want the freedom to say yes or no.	You're trying to run my life.
I want respectful friendship with you again.	You've got to respect me or you're not my friend.

Building Relationships

▶ Relationship-Building Exercises

The purpose of these exercises is to build the relationships in your group by encouraging fun, communication, honesty, transparency, authenticity, and shared experiences. As relationships grow, community will be enhanced.

"... *if you had a tumor and your doctor, having examined you, had determined that it was malignant, would you want him to ignore telling you the hard truth? ... If we want the truth from those who watch over our physical condition, how much more should we want the truth from those who watch over our souls.*"

Chuck Swindoll
Dropping Your Guard

"He is able" celebration

Ask your group members to bring to your next meeting a tangible item that represents how God has proven Himself able in their own lives recently. Ask them to be prepared to explain how God has been able, and how that item represents God's ability to act and bless.

- It should be a physical item that they can hold up and talk about

- They should talk about their own experience (not someone else's)

- Ask them to relate a recent experience that they have had

At the meeting, let each person relate their story. You may wish to close this time by all singing the song, "He Is Able."

Variation: "God Answers Prayer" celebration

"Remember when"

In the Scriptures, we often see God's people recounting the past experiences they have had or remembering God's deeds. This can be done in a variety of ways.

- Remember how you first heard about Christianity

- Give your testimonies

- Remember times when God answered prayer

- Remember when God brought you through a difficult situation

- If your group has been together for a while, remember things you have been through together, and what they meant to you

- Retell the story of first coming to your church and explain what the church has meant to you

This experience builds a sense of "history" with your group if you've been together for a while. Recounting God's character or your experiences can be a prelude to a time of worship.

Two truths/One lie

Give everyone in the group a sheet of paper and a pen or marker. Have everyone write down two true things about themselves and one lie. These can be in any order. (Have them write big enough so the paper can be shown and seen around the room.) Then have someone read their three items. Everyone must guess which item is a lie. The person then reads each item and explains why it is a truth or a lie. Have everyone take a turn.

Questions in a hat

Before your meeting, fill a hat (or bowl) with opener questions on individual pieces of paper (one question on each piece of paper). Have at least as many questions as there are people in the group. Vary the depth of the questions to be appropriate for your group. Add the following "special" things on separate pieces of paper and put them in the hat:

"Pass to the Right"

"Pass to the Left"

"Boomerang (back to you)"

At the beginning, state that everyone always has the right to "pass" on any question (to put people at ease and not feel put on the spot). Someone (let's say Mary) picks a question out of the hat. Mary can ask anyone in the room (but just one person) to answer that question. She asks John. After John answers the question, he then picks a question and asks anyone in the room *except* Mary, and so on.

If you pulled the "Pass to the right" or "Pass to the left" pieces out of the hat, save them and use them when you are asked a question. If you use a "Pass to the right," then the person on your right must answer the question. If you have the "Boomerang," then the person who asked you the question must answer it. (Of course, anyone can pass if they wish.)

"Who am I?"

During the week before your meeting, collect one unknown fact about everyone in the group. This should be something the group members will not mind being told. The leader types a list of these facts (including one for himself/herself). Enough copies are made so everyone has a list.

At the meeting, the lists are handed out. The objective is to find out which fact matches which person. You may approach someone and ask about only two items on the list. ("Are you the one who. . ." If not, then "Are you the one who . . ."). After two inquiries, you must move on to someone else.

After a time limit (or as soon as someone gets them all), the game stops and you read through the list, identifying everyone.

Draw a time line of your life

Give everyone a long sheet of paper and pens or markers. Have each group member draw a time line of his or her life, showing three to five major life events. The number of events can vary, depending upon how much time you have. Then let each explain what he or she drew.

Draw a self-portrait

Give everyone a large sheet of paper and markers or crayons. Have each person draw a self-portrait. Collect all the self-portraits, hold them up one by one, and guess who each represents. When you figure out who it is, have that person tell a little about themselves.

Introductions

When introductions are needed, instead of everyone introducing themselves, let someone else in the group introduce them. If it is a couple's group, have the spouses introduce each other. This can be very affirming.

Videos

Videos can be used for times of worship, praise, or singing. Or use a home video camera to film "A Day in the Life" of a group member.

Subgrouping

If your group is large enough, break them up into smaller groups, even pairs, for various activities. This is especially useful for times of prayer, sharing on a personal level, allowing relationships to deepen, and dealing with sensitive subjects.

Names of God

Ask, "What attribute of God has been especially meaningful to you lately?" (For example, "I really appreciate God's faithfulness to me because . . .")

Have the leader and each person in the group talk about this.

Variation: Don't talk about it—go right to prayer and pray through it.

Their names in a verse

The leader, ahead of time, picks a topic, and chooses verses on that topic—one verse for each member of the group and for him- or herself. During prayer time, have each person read his or her assigned verse with their own name in it and pray through that verse.

For example, the topic is "God's love for us." Verses chosen could be Psalm 13:5–6, John 15:9, Romans 5:5, etc. One of the group members, Mary, reads aloud Psalm 13:5–6: "But I, Mary, trust in your unfailing love; my heart rejoices in your salvation. I, Mary, will sing to you Lord, for you have been good to me."

Serve each other

Look for opportunities to serve each other outside of group time. This will really go a long way in developing your relationships with each other. How about

- painting someone's house (inside or out)

- doing a large cleaning project

- bringing meals when help is needed

Serving others together

Look for opportunities to serve as a group, providing help, support, or encouragement to someone else. Here are a things you can do:

- help a needy family or person(s)

- serve at church for a special event (i.e., childcare for Easter service)

- look into an international ministries opportunity

Celebrate

Search for things to celebrate: groups starting, birthing, growing; personal accomplishments; the end of a season of your group; a successful experience. Be creative in the way you celebrate. Enjoy being together!

"It's a wonderful life"

In advance, the leader secretly asks three close friends (may include the spouse) of each group member to write out what the world would be like if that person had never been born. Before reading these aloud, the leader cues up the scene from the classic movie when George Bailey tells the angel it would be better if he had never lived, and the angel Clarence has an idea to show him how the world would have suffered.

After viewing the video, read the three letters aloud for each person. Allow time for the group to comment.

Gauges

Each person is given a white sheet of cardboard. These have been prepared in advance with the following categories on the left margin:

Emotional	*(Am I in touch with my feelings?)*
Relational	*(What is the quality of my family relationships and friendships?)*
Physical/Recreational	*(Am I healthy? Am I having any fun?)*
Ministry Fulfillment	*(What is my joy level in ministry?)*
Spiritual	*(How honest and growing is my relationship with God these days?)*

Colored pieces of tape or colored markers are then made available. Each person takes time to analyze each dimension of his or her life and put a piece of tape or wide band of color next to each gauge. Colors have the following meanings:

Green	I am flourishing in this area.
Gray	I am doing okay; nothing too great, nothing too bad.
Yellow	I have growing concerns for this area. Caution!
Red	I am in trouble in this area. It requires serious attention and correction.

Then each person holds up their card and explains the gauges.

Hot seat

The leader calls each group member, one at a time, to sit on a seat in the room, facing everyone. Then the person on the hot seat chooses a question from a pile and answers it. Members of the group pose follow-up questions or discuss the person's responses for the next three to four minutes.

Sample questions for the above exercise might include:

What is your favorite book of the Bible and why?

Fill in the blank:

Lately I am becoming more _____.

The feeling that best describes where I am at right now is _____.

If there was one person in the world that I could spend a day with, that would be _____.

Group member appreciation night

Each member of the group has a piece of paper with their name at the top of it. Lines are drawn on the paper to create enough boxes for all of the people in the room. At the top of the sheet is the sentence, "I appreciate this person because he/she . . ." Pass these sheets around the room, asking each member to complete the sentence by filling in one box. After all the sheets have been passed to everyone in the room, return the sheets to their owners. Then have members share what impresses them most about the affirmation they received from others in the group. (This will take approximately 30–45 minutes.)

Life story

Over the period of several weeks, each member of the small group can be assigned to spend fifteen minutes telling his or her life story. Then, fifteen minutes of discussion and interacting can occur. The point of the exercise is to find out exactly where people have come from. Often, it is hard to appreciate people until we understand their past and some of the significant events in their lives.

Group communion service

The purpose of this is to share in the Bread and the Cup as a small group. This can be an incredibly meaningful experience.

Each person, one at a time, personally serves another group member. (You can assign whom they will serve in advance or simply move around the circle.) As you serve one another, make appropriate comments about the love of Christ, specifically for that individual. When you are completed, the group closes in a time of prayer and/or worship.

Three key material possessions

Set up the scene as follows: Explain to the group that they have just discovered a major fire in their home. Assuming they have been able to safely get their family out, what three *material* possessions would they take with them from their burning home? Have members explain why they would take the items they chose. Then generate a discussion to discover the value behind each of these possessions and why we hold certain possessions so dear.

Group photo

The purpose of this exercise is to have each member take a "picture" of the group. In other words, have each person draw or describe what the group looks like using a word-picture. For example, the group could be described as any of the following:

- A hospital (a place where wounds are healed)

- A gas station (a place to be refueled spiritually)

- A fortress (a safe place where struggles can be shared)

- A battleground (a place where we can work on who we are becoming in Christ)

- A mountaintop (a place to gain perspective and be encouraged)

- A valley (a place of discouragement and trial)

- A carnival (a place for fun, enthusiasm, and excitement)

These are just some examples, but have members either draw or describe the kind of group environment they need or see.

Fill in the blank

Ask various members of the group the following "fill in the blank" questions:

1. Tomorrow, something I will most likely take for granted is

   _____

   _____

2. Last year at this time I never would have thought God would

   _____

3. The person I am most thankful for this year is _____ because he/she

   _____

   _____

4. One specific attribute of God which I most appreciate is that He is

   _____

   _____

5. The following people have been especially used by the Lord to enrich my life this past year:

   _____

   _____

6. I want to specifically thank the Lord for giving me the gift of _____, so I can use it to serve Him and the church.

7. Considering the standard of living of most of the world's population, I am rich because I have these material blessings:

   _____

   _____

"We are living in an era when the art of conversation is almost a thing of the past . . . Yet at the same time, there is a growing hunger for closeness, for being known and understood."

Jerry Jones
201 Great Questions

8. If I could stand up and shout anything to the rest of the body tonight, I would tell them that:

_____

_____

9. My God is _____.

▶ Ideas for Worship

1. Listen to or sing along with a worship tape.

2. Walk through a nearby park or forest preserve and praise God for His creative power.

3. Ask your group to think of the names of God that are found in Scripture. Ask each member to tell why that name is important, and pause to give God glory for who He is.

4. Ask members to select a favorite psalm or Scripture passage that focuses on who God is or who Jesus is. Read it aloud and then pause to pray.

5. Have each member write prayers of worship and praise to God. Ask them to share them with the group. Think of this as writing a letter to God.

6. Go to a worshipful Christian concert or church service together.

7. Have members in your group use their video cameras (if they have one) to record images of things that cause them to think about God or to want to worship Him. View them together as a group. Pause to reflect upon who God is and what He is doing in your lives.

▶ Social Activities

1. Eat meals together.

2. Play sports together.

3. Take a retreat as a group.

4. Go to a park.

5. Go to a concert.

6. Go to a lake/beach for the day.

7. Go to someplace special at Christmas time.

8. Go to a pumpkin patch at Thanksgiving.

9. Have a fall harvest party.

10. Watch a video together and critique it.

11. Make popcorn, ice cream, or pizza together.

12. Brainstorm with your group some fun things to do.

▶ Outreach

1. Pray for someone to fill the open chair.

2. Pray for different parts of the world that need Christ.

3. Pray for a missionary from the church.

4. Plan a trip to the inner city.

5. Gather materials or gifts together to present to an orphanage in America or Mexico.

6. Have a potluck dinner and invite visitors.

7. Have a Superbowl party and invite neighbors.

8. Adopt a child through World Vision and support that child financially.

9. Plan to bring friends to a seeker service.

10. Take the *Becoming a Contagious Christian* training course together.

With all these exercises, please remember:

- Know your goal.

- Think through the group size and break it down into smaller groups if necessary.

- Make sure you allow enough time for everyone and don't shorten the time required.

- The leader must participate like everyone else.

- Let the Spirit move and don't get in the way. Be discerning about when to step in or redirect and when to just be quiet. Face the awkwardness of the expression of emotions.

Troubleshooting Tips

Creating safe places where life change can be maximized is not easy. Sometimes it's reassuring to know that all small groups undergo some type of relational difficulty. If group members expect to grow, people will have to be vulnerable. Anyone who has ever led or been a part of a nurturing small group will tell you that where people are emotionally transparent, problems will come to the surface. When they do, it's the leader's job to help steer the group in the right direction.

Two principles guide a leader's attempts at successful troubleshooting. First, any solution must promote the health and wholeness of the individual. Second, any resolution must also promote the health and wholeness of the total group.

The following troubleshooting tips were garnered in part from discussions with leaders. They should go a long way in helping your group deal with problem situations with grace and insight. Remember, no technique is 100 percent successful in solving the crisis your group may encounter, but with prayerful attention, sensitivity, and caring interaction using one or more of these tips, your group has a good chance of not only making it through your particular barrier, but realizing true community and maturity on the other side of it.

►Issue #1— The Overly Talkative Member

If not moderated properly, what often begins as a trickle of friendly patter can turn into a virtual flood of words. The Talker is rarely shy, and usually very uncomfortable with long periods of silence. Typically, what's behind this need to fill in the pauses is the fear of intimacy or personal disclosure. The Talker is very quick to move on an item and can very easily unsettle a group's pacing if there is not some type of sensitive intervention. Here are some tools that you may find helpful.

Establish ground rules for your group

- Set the rule that no one can speak a second time unless everyone who wants to talk has had a chance to speak. Often in the case of a Talker who is married, the spouse is silent or appears introverted. Use the situation to your advantage. Each person may speak a second time only after their spouse has been given an opportunity. You would be amazed at the positive response from overrun mates.

- Make (or reiterate) the rule that no one can overrun someone else while they are speaking (translation: "NO INTERRUPTING!").

- Go systematically around the group, allowing each person a chance to talk. Remember at the onset to be sensitive with members who are either unaccustomed to or feel uncomfortable with speaking in a group setting.

- Assure the talkative member privately that you value his or her sharing but that you wish to hear other people's comments as well. In front of the group, state that you would like to hear more about the person's items of interest after the meeting.

- Agree at the beginning of the meeting to save some issues for the end, after everything else has been discussed (this only works after you have seen the Talker verbally camp on certain subjects repeatedly).

- Here's a creative solution: throw a football or some other object around the room. Only the person with the object in his or her hand has the right to talk in the group.

- During the discussion, simply interject and sensitively direct a question to another person.

Meet individually

- Spend some one-on-one time with the Talker. Attempt to ascertain the driving issues that are making it necessary for the person to dominate the meeting.

- Firmly and sensitively confront the person in private. Begin with the positive contributions the person has made in the group and the need for others to be given the opportunity to make a similar impact. Use the confrontation time as an important affirmation moment as well.

- Ask for the Talker's help in drawing others out. Suggest he or she end his or her comments with a question like, "So what do the rest of you think?"

▶ Issue #2—The Answer Person

For too many years within the Christian community, spiritual fruitfulness has been wrongly determined on the basis of how much you know. This measure stands in sharp contrast to the biblical notion that "fruit" for the believer is defined by what you do and by who you are. Because of this misinterpretation of Jesus' teaching, knowledge has preceded action on the list of preeminent Christlike virtues. It is not hard to see, then, why many sincere group members see nothing wrong with throwing around easy answers, simply quoting a Bible verse, or becoming wrapped up in some minute theological trivia having nothing to do with the group discussion. These group members are often argumentative and have very little tolerance for outside interpretation of feelings or biblical passages. They often will go to great lengths to make sure their opinions are heard and validated.

Answer people all too quickly dismantle safe places. Other members should not have to experience the pain of non-attention, judgment, or an argumentative spirit. Here are some helpful ways to provide what the Answer person needs and keep the group process on track.

Take action during the meeting

- Backtrack to the original idea, question, or thought shared.

- Refocus on the passage or material being used and collect more information from everyone; then summarize.

- Lovingly redirect the discussion to the other group members: "What do the rest of you think of this passage?" or "How do the rest of you feel?"

- Affirm what is right about the "always right" person's answers, but look for other points of view.

- Be a model of true empathy yourself so the Answer person can see a better way to help others.

- Remind the group of the importance of silence.

- Avoid arguing about who is right or wrong.

- Before the meeting, share how "pat" answers or oversimplified responses make others feel. Ask the group to monitor themselves. Do not feel afraid to call members on this after you have set the ground rules.

- Direct the group to prayer.

Speak to the Answer person

- If it's a continuing problem, talk with the person outside the group. Describe to them what their sharing in this manner does to the group. Tell the truth in love.

- Affirm the person for what they do know, but also let them know how their knowledge may not be what is needed or appropriate.

- Let the person know they need to let the communication of others stand on its own without judgment or immediate correction.

- Ask the insensitive member to share more feelings rather than thoughts ("I think . . .").

- Ask the Answer person to help summarize or rephrase points of the discussion.

- Attempt to find out from the person privately what drives him or her to always appear "in the know."

► Issue #3—
The Member with an Agenda

All of us struggle from time to time with the issue of wanting to maintain inordinate control over aspects of our lives. Groups can become the arena where our sinful power struggles play out. Some individuals will be especially prone to repeatedly trying to prove themselves and will try to redirect some facet of group life their way for no apparent reason other than their own preferences.

A person presenting this problem leaves telltale language clues. Look for phrases such as "yes, but" or "Well, I think." Often this person is critical of the group process, even with items considered tabled by the group. Here are some hints to aid you in dealing with this individual.

Reaffirm group covenants while you're all together

- Reaffirm, recast, reestablish, challenge, redefine—use whatever word you want, but remind everyone of the agreed upon guidelines for group involvement.

- Discuss these standards with everyone in the group to affirm the purpose and values of the gathering.

Speak to the person with the agenda

- Confront the person privately and attempt to discern the underlying problem.

- Suggest that the person work with the other members to find a proactive solution that solves the problem yet doesn't violate the boundary established by the group.

▶ Issue #4—Superficial Discussions

Beginning relationships often have a period where facts are shared more easily than feelings. Not much is bartered in terms of emotional risk and therefore not much is gained at this stage. Early on, this surface-level communication is normal and shouldn't be cause for alarm.

Often though, a group struggles to break through the strong ice of superficiality and go deeper, even after many meetings. This hesitation can be the result of a leader's direction, or because someone else is impeding progress in group members' bonding. Whatever is keeping the group in a "functionally frozen" mode, you can easily prepare yourself to handle this problem.

Surface communication can also be a sign that you are attempting to go too deep too fast. Mentally take a step back and ascertain whether this is so. If you sense you have gone too quickly, admit your error and be willing to proceed at a more realistic pace. By humbling yourself in this way, you model vulnerability rather than harming the relational chemistry of those gathered. Your openness actually works to center the focus and unite the participants for future growth together.

Improve your questions

- By far, the number one way to open up a group is to lead by example. "Speed of the leader, speed of the team," could easily have been first postulated in a small group. Usual rule of thumb is to speak as deeply and openly as you would like the others to share.

- Have specific applications and questions. Don't be afraid to challenge the group.

- Ask "feeling" questions rather than just "opinion" or "fact" questions.

- Where appropriate, be more directive. Sometimes ask closed-ended questions that will elicit specific answers rather than open-ended questions.

- Restate and rephrase the question. Often silence means group members are simply unsure of what was asked of them. (Silence may also indicate they're thinking, not that they're reluctant.)

Create a safer climate

- During initial minutes of the meeting, remind members of confidentiality guidelines.

- If your group is too large, break into smaller sub-groups.

- Contact the group members outside of the meeting to see if anything could have made the questions easier to answer.

Meeting Follow-up

Gaining Feedback for Your Ministry

The purpose of all feedback and evaluation is improvement and increased effectiveness for your ministry. Gaining feedback from others about your leadership and about your group is designed to help you build on your strengths and buttress your weaknesses.

We have designed three tools that will help you evaluate and improve your small group ministry. The tools are described on the chart below and samples of those tools are included. Get the actual forms from your ministry leaders.

Tools for Evaluating Your Ministry

Form	Purpose	Required or Optional	Completed by	How often
Touching Base (TB) form *(Meetings)*	To summarize meeting activity, apprentice development, future plans, specific prayer requests and celebrations	Required	Apprentice and/or Leader	Monthly
Leader Feedback and Development *(Leader)*	To help leaders build on strengths and improve areas requiring skill development	Optional	Apprentice, Members, or Coach	As desired (at least twice per year)
Planning for Life Change *(Group)*	To help groups discuss their growth and maturity as a group	Optional	Leader and group together	Every six months

Touching Base—Small Group Summary

Leader _____   Month _____ Year _____

Apprentice Leader[1] _____   Coach _____

Apprentice Leader[2] _____   Division Leader/Ministry Director _____

Instructions: Leaders, please fill out this form each month. Keep your copy, then pass a copy on to your Coach or Ministry Director.

Attendance Record

Meetings:	Date 1	Date 2	Date 3	Date 4		Summary
Total Attendance (total # at meeting)					AVG=	
Primary Care Attenders					AVG=	
First Time Visitors					AVG=	
Guest (ex: Coach, div. leader, friend of member)					TOT=	
Regular Attenders Absent					AVG=	

Has anyone left your group over the past month? ☐ Yes ☐ No If yes, please provide their name and reason for leaving.

Name   Reason for leaving

_____   _____

_____   _____

Activity Summary Briefly describe what your group did this month; include in-group, out-of-group, and one-on-one activities.

Next Steps What are your plans for the group for the next month? What are you doing to develop your apprentice(s)? Have you identified any potential apprentices?

Just To Let You Know... Is there anything you'd like to celebrate? Do you have any problems, prayer requests, or questions? *(Note: For urgent problems or prayer requests, please call your Coach or division leader.)*

Leadership Feedback and Development (Part 1)

From: _____

Please note: This tool is designed to evaluate for the purpose of encouragement, not to judge for the purpose of condemnation.

Leadership during meetings

1. On a continuum, how would you rate the leader's style of communication during the meetings? Mark with an "X":

_____

Pure lecture   *Pure discussion*

On the scale above, mark with an "O" where you would like the leader to be.

2. On a continuum, how would rate the leader's control of the flow of the meetings? Mark with an "X":

_____

Autocratic/Control   *Collaboration/Relaxed*

On the same scale above, mark with an "O" where you would like the leader to be.

3. On a continuum, how would you rate the group members' overall participation in discussions? Mark with an "X":

_____

A vocal minority   *Balanced participation*

What, if anything, could the leader do about the balance of participation?

4. How did the leader handle the different elements of the meeting?

   - Starting on time

   - Homework review (if applicable)

   - Scripture explanation or teaching

   - Discussion portions

   - Helping to make personal applications

   - Ending on time

Leadership Outside the Meetings (Part 2)

1. What experiences with the leader outside the regular meeting times have been especially valuable to you?

2. What aspects of the leader's life do you most need (want) to observe so you can see a godly example?

3. What steps could your leader take beyond leading the regular group meetings to help you grow (be specific)?

4. Comment on the leader in the following areas:

   • Availability outside of group times

   • Approachability and concern

   • Keeping me accountable and being firm if necessary

   • Sensitivity and compassion

5. Is there any other feedback you would like to give the leader?

6. Are there issues that are unresolved or require attention?

7. What affirmation can you give the leader—what aspect of the whole small group experience has been especially meaningful to you?

8. How will you pray for the leader?

Planning for Life Change

Date: _____

Leader: _____

How Are We Doing?

Evaluation Scale
3 *Doing well; pleased with results*
2 *Going in the right direction; see areas for improvement*
1 *Struggling; need help*

Our Group Is...

Maturing Spiritually

☐ Group members are spiritual self-starters and are actively developing their relationship with God. They are participating in the church through the use of their spiritual gifts and material resources.

Comments:

Growing Relationally

☐ Group members are actively building relationships with each other both inside and outside of group setting.

Comments:

Fostering Safety

☐ The group is a safe place where all members willingly share their thoughts and feelings in a straight forward and transparent manner.

Comments:

Generating Excitement

☐ Group meetings are full of life and energy. Members look forward to coming and consistently mention how the group meetings are one of the highlights of their week.

Comments:

Welcoming Outsiders

☐ Group members invite unconnected people. The open chair is utilized, and new members are being brought into the group at a rate of at least two regular attenders per every 24 meetings.

Comments:

Preparing to Birth

☐ The group embraces the value of needing to birth, and new leaders (apprentices and host/hostess) are being recruited and developed to ensure healthy daughter groups.

Comments:

Resources

Commonly Asked Questions about Conducting Meetings

Q *How long should a good meeting last?*

A Long enough to engage the group; short enough to create a longing to return again. Don't feel like you have to bring every meeting to perfect closure. Let members leave a meeting with some unanswered questions. It will keep them interested for days!

Q *Where is the best location for our meeting?*

A It depends on the purpose. Ask yourself, "Where can we meet to make this a memorable time and fulfill our purpose?" Variety keeps a group fresh. A change in location will often produce a change in attentiveness, participation, and openness.

Additional Resources

How to Lead Small Groups by Neil McBride (NavPress)
> Chapter 7, "Evaluating Your Group," has some helpful information and important questions for any group leader to think through. Though the evaluation methods discussed are not the same as ours, the material is thought-provoking.

Small Group Leader's Handbook by a small group (InterVarsity)
> Chapter 12 is an excellent chapter for group activities and ideas.

Shepherding Members

Making Disciples

Group-Based Discipleship

Discipleship is often misunderstood as a primarily one-on-one adventure. But in the New Testament, making disciples has always been a group event. As we stated earlier, the Scriptures rarely record our Lord meeting with fewer than three of the twelve disciples. One-on-one disciplemaking in the context of group life protects the newer disciple from becoming a clone of any one member. Rather, it allows disciples to grow in Christ by experiencing the teaching, mentoring, love, encouragement, exhortation, and giftedness of many brothers and sisters in Christ.

So when do we do one-on-one ministry? As we look at one-on-one encounters between Jesus and Peter, Paul and Timothy, and Paul and Silas, it is clear these are leadership development relationships, not basic discipleship. It *is* important to spend time training rising leaders. However, most of the time you can accomplish disciplemaking goals through group-based discipleship. Ministry in and through groups and teams more adequately reflects the New Testament model (Mark 3:14; Matt. 10:5–42; Acts 13:2; Acts 16:1–5) and creates an environment of mutual support, ministry, accountability, and training.

Promoting Spiritual Growth

Spiritual growth is a process that requires time and a willing spirit. It results from the work of the Holy Spirit, obedience to the Word, intimacy with Christ, and having experiences (especially adversity) and accountable relationships in community. As a group leader, you do not *cause* spiritual growth, but you can create an environment that promotes and facilitates such growth. That's why we have stressed the importance of using the Word of God in your group, teaching your group to pray, understanding the role of the Holy Spirit in your group, and the need to build authentic, lasting relationships with members.

One of the best ways to foster the spiritual growth of group members is to gauge the group's spiritual growth using the 5 G's. As previously noted, The Five G's— grace, growth, group, gifts, and good stewardship—reflect a discipleship process.

A Shepherding Plan has been developed using these Five G's so that you can "grow your group" in Christ. As you work through the Scriptures and questions together, this Shepherding Plan becomes a disciplemaking tool.

Use the worksheet and chart found below to help you develop a strategy for facilitating spiritual growth in your group members. Sit down with each member of your group and help them identify areas of spiritual growth that need attention such as Bible study, prayer, relationships, past wounds, serving, good stewardship, et cetera. Then, as you meet with individual members over the life span of the group, follow up with them by using this chart to help you remember your goals and guidelines for group growth.

Small Group Leader Shepherding Plan for Making Disciples

Leader's Name _____   Quarter: 1 2 3 4

		Group Development Plan	
		Questions	**Quarterly Plan**
	Grace To experience and extend saving grace. (2 Cor. 5:18–19)	• Who can we pray for to receive Christ? • How can we encourage and equip each other to extend saving grace to our families, friends, coworkers, neighbors, or world for Christ? • How can we team up in our evangelistic efforts?	
	Growth To grow in having Christ spiritually formed in us. (Heb. 10:24–25)	• What are the practices, experiences, and relationships that will help form Christ in our group? • What will we study to form Christ in each other? • How can we foster participation in worship together?	
	Groups To shepherd one another in loving, authentic community. (Gal. 6:2)	• How can we better love, care for, and be the body of Christ to one another? • How can we foster greater authenticity, vulnerability, and openness? • What's the next step in extending or multiplying our loving community to others?	
	Gifts To discover, develop, and deploy our spiritual gifts to serve the body of Christ. (Rom. 12:6–8)	• How can we serve the body of Christ together? • How can we help develop and deploy each other's spiritual gifts? • What church "household chores" can we help with as a group?	
	Good Stewardship To steward our time and treasures for God's redemptive purposes in our church, community, nation, and world. (Matt. 25:40)	• How can we encourage each other to better steward our time and treasures? • How can our group extend compassion locally and globally? • What unique personal, spiritual, or material resources do we have to share?	

Encouraging Group Members

Encouragement takes place when your love meets a member's fear. Everyone has fears or disappointments or confusion about life. When we show others that we truly love them in the midst of their pain, we are providing encouragement. Proverbs 18:21 tells us that death and life are in the power of the tongue. Encouraging words bring life; shaming or harsh words bring death. Your job as a leader is to bring words of life to people who are feeling the sting of death emotionally. Listen to the instructions of Paul in Ephesians 4:29: "Do not let any unwholesome talk come out of your mouths, but only what is helpful for building others up according to their needs, that it may benefit those who listen." Encouragement is a community builder.

▶ Tips for Becoming an Encouraging Small Group Leader

1. **Be slow to speak** (Prov. 12:18; 13:3; James 1:19). A great way to encourage members is to listen to their stories with attentiveness and caring. Do not try to fix things quickly or give glib, pat answers to their problems or issues. Simply listen.

2. **Exercise sensitivity.** The Bible reminds us that our speech should be seasoned with salt. Our words should be filled with grace (Eph. 4:29) and should mimic those of Jesus who came in grace and truth (John 1:14).

3. **Show kindness when you speak.** Words of gentleness are soothing and tender. Truth does not always have to be delivered from a rifle barrel. Truth spoken gently is more readily heard and more easily obeyed.

▶ Pitfalls to Avoid When Trying to Be an Encourager

1. **Defensiveness.** Don't try to justify yourself. Simply listen to what others are saying and try to clarify what is being said.

2. **Sarcasm and criticism.** Sometimes humor gets out of hand. Remember that people are easily wounded with words (Prov. 15:4).

3. **Correction.** Don't tell people that their feelings are wrong or inaccurate or say to someone, "You shouldn't feel that way." The point is, they do feel that way, and you need to listen carefully to determine why they have the feelings they are experiencing.

4. **Advice-giving.** Avoid giving answers before having really investigated the questions. Advice-giving can be patronizing and can shut down communication. Quick advice often ignores the real problem.

"It is our responsibility as Christians to tune in to the possible impact of our words in every situation and to select only those that reflect a sensitivity to the needs of others."

Larry Crabb
Encouragement

Real encouragement requires active listening. It means fully engaging with another person and participating in their pain and frustration. As you listen carefully, you will be able to bring words of encouragement and comfort and hope to people in your group. Remember, the Scriptures are full of exhortations and commands to build up and encourage one another. The following "one anothers" of the New Testament reveal the heart of God and His desire for His people to develop deep, caring relationships with one another. As you study them, reflect upon how you might incorporate them into your group's activities.

Some of the "One Anothers" of the New Testament

Be at peace with one another (Mark 9:50)

Love one another (John 13:34)

Be devoted to one another (Rom. 12:10)

Honor one another (Rom. 12:10)

Live in harmony with one another (Rom. 12:16)

Stop passing judgment on one another (Rom. 14:13)

Accept one another (Rom. 15:7)

Instruct one another (Rom. 15:14)

Greet one another (Rom. 16:16)

Serve one another (Gal. 5:13)

Carry each other's burden (Gal. 6:2)

Be patient, bearing with one another in love (Eph. 4:2)

Be kind and compassionate to one another (Eph. 4:32)

Forgive each other (Eph. 4:32)

Speak to one another with psalms, hymns and spiritual songs (Eph. 5:19)

Submit to one another out of reverence for Christ (Eph. 5:21)

In humility consider others better than yourselves (Phil. 2:3)

Teach one another (Col. 3:16)

Admonish one another (Col. 3:16)

Encourage each other (1 Thess. 4:18)

Build each other up (1 Thess. 5:11)

Spur one another on toward love and good deeds (Heb. 10:24)

Do not slander one another (James 4:11)

Don't grumble against each other (James 5:9)

Confess your sins to each other (James 5:16)

Pray for one another (James 5:16)

Clothe yourselves with humility toward one another (1 Peter 5:5)

Providing Care

Caregiving and Shepherding

Giving care is part of the role of being a shepherd. God expects us to give the kind of care that He Himself would give to His flock. This is clear from Ezekiel 34:1–16, in which God rebukes the shepherds of Israel for not giving appropriate care to the flock. As you study the passage, you see that God desires shepherds to

- feed the flock

- lead them to rest

- seek the lost

- bring back the scattered

- bind up the broken

- strengthen the sick

Being a shepherd is an awesome responsibility. That is why we have limited the leader's span of care. If you have too many people to care for, you will eventually burn out. How much care do you provide and how often? There are three levels of *fundamental* caregiving: primary care, mutual care, and backup care. Crisis or *emergency* caregiving is discussed in the next section.

▶ Primary Care

Primary care is the normal, regular attention and support that a small group leader is expected to provide for group members. Sometimes people belong to more than one group. In such cases, ask them to identify where they expect to receive primary care. Such care includes prayer support, phone calls, encouragement, visiting the sick, and finding resources that will meet group members' care needs.

▶Mutual Care

Mutual care is what group members give to one another. It is not possible (nor expected) for a small group leader to provide all the care for all the members of the group. It is the goal of a small group to provide mutual, interactive care for one another. This kind of care includes taking meals to families with new babies, visiting those in the hospital, and providing prayer and assistance with other needs. Such care enables us to fulfill the commandment in Galatians 6:2, where it says, "Carry each other's burdens, and in this way you will fulfill the law of Christ."

▶Backup Care

Your first line of defense, or backup care, is your coach. If your coach is unavailable, contact your division leader or other church leader. Together you can work out a "care strategy" for the particular need that you are seeking to meet.

Responding to a Crisis

Crisis Caregiving

From time to time in a small group, an emergency or crisis may occur. As a small group leader, others will look to you in times of crisis.

▶ Handling a Crisis

In cases of impending physical danger

Contact the police immediately. Such crises would include:

- Life-threatening situations

- Severe accidents or emergencies

- An attempted suicide or threatened suicide

- Present threats of violence by a person to him- or herself or to others

Though it is very unlikely that you would ever experience any of these in the context of a group meeting (or even with members of your group), please be aware of the possibility and know that you should contact the police immediately.

Other serious situations

If you have a serious situation that may require further help and guidance to address (e.g., child abuse or neglect, spousal abuse, et cetera), contact your coach and church immediately for help in discerning the severity of the crisis and for assistance in reporting the incident to the proper authorities (if needed).

Remember, in most situations, your first point of contact should be your coach. If your coach is unavailable, contact your division leader or other ministry leader. But if there is any threat of violence or danger, call the police immediately.

▶Supporting vs. Counseling

As a small group leader, you are expected to provide support and encouragement to members of your group. However, you are not trained to be a professional counselor, so you should not assume such a role. Instead, your responsibility is to provide opportunities for your members to receive the appropriate care they require. Situations that may require professional help:

- Serious marriage problems

- History of past abuse

- Addictions

- Severe personality disorders

- Mental disorders or dysfunctions

If you should encounter anything that resembles the examples above, contact your coach to see what steps should be taken. Together you can determine a plan for encouraging a group member to participate in counseling or another type of help. Never contact a church leader directly and give a member's name to them. In such cases, it is imperative that you do not violate a person's right to confidentiality.

Just because you think someone is in need of counseling does not mean they will be willing to participate in counseling. Work with your coach and with ministry leaders at the church to determine how to approach an individual with the suggestion of counseling or other help.

Resources

Commonly Asked Questions about Shepherding Members

Q *What if I am not competent to meet the needs of my group?*

A All too often, leaders feel obligated to meet every members' need. And when they fail, they feel guilty. You will often need the support of your coach, the staff, and other group members in order to meet members' needs. Let it be a team effort!

Q *My personality type does not do well with confrontation. What do I do?*

A One way or another, you will have to face the truth. Ignoring an unpleasant situation will only make it worse. Stuffing feeling and emotions will eventually lead to an emotional blowup. Better to enter the tunnel of confronation voluntarily, choosing your words wisely, to remedy the situation before things get worse.

Q *Does an official membership program help the small group ministry?*

A Interestingly, we have found a small group ministry enhances the membership efforts of the church. Small groups are a strategic place to cast vision and ask for commitment. Our entire membership process has been decentralized to the small group leaders and coaches, under the supervision of the elders. Small group members, we've discovered, are the most commited people at our church as evidenced by their service, attendance, giving, and participation in the life of the body.

Additional Resources

Caring Enough to Confront by David Augsburger (Herald Press)

Encouragement by Lawrence Crabb Jr. and Dan B. Allender (Zondervan)

Lifestyle Discipleship by Jim Petersen (NavPress)

Telling Each Other the Truth by William Backus (Bethany House)

Part Seven

Multiplying Your Ministry

Adding Members to Your Group

Group Multiplication

▶ God and the Open Chair

Since the beginning of time, it has been God's desire to create a people who would have fellowship with Him for all eternity. Though He enjoyed perfect fellowship as a tri-unity (Father, Son, Holy Spirit), God's desire was to expand that community to all who put their faith in Him. From Genesis to Revelation, we see God's heart in reaching people and including them in this new community:

The promise of a Messiah (Gen. 3:15)

The promise to Noah (Gen. 9:8–17)

The promise to Abraham to make him a great nation (Gen. 12:1–5)

God's promise to make the Israelites His people (Ex. 6:7)

God's promise to David of an eternal kingdom and a place for God's people to dwell (2 Sam. 7:1–17)

God desires to be known among all nations of the earth (Ps. 67)

The invitation for all to come and be part of God's community (Isa. 55:1–3)

The promise of a Messiah who would become known throughout the earth (Mic. 5:2–5)

God will be known among all the nations of the earth (Zeph. 3:8–10, 20)

The invitation for all to come and receive Christ (Matt. 11:28–30)

The command to make disciples of all nations (Matt. 28:18–20)

The promise that all who believe will become part of a new community (John 3:16)

The power of the Holy Spirit will enable all to witness for Christ (Acts 1:8)

The world will not hear the Gospel unless we take it to them (Rom. 10:14–15)

As you can see, our God has been inviting people into His "open chair" for centuries. This is evident in a personal way in the life of Jesus. Jesus used the concept of the open chair to develop relationships with Nicodemus, the woman at the well, the woman caught in adultery, and the twelve disciples—and His invitation continues today. Andrew opened the chair for Peter, Barnabas opened the chair for Paul, and Paul opened the chair for Timothy. Part of discipleship is opening the chair to those who are not involved in biblical community. This includes seekers, fringe Christians, and committed believers who are seeking fellowship.

▶ Filling the Open Chair

Many of you may be asking, "How do I fill the open chair?" Here are some steps to think through and a chart that will help you brainstorm the names of people who could potentially be added to your group.

Step 1: Before you begin inviting new members

A. Involve everyone in the process. Everyone in your group should invite people to the group.

B. Teach your group about the open chair.

C. Regularly pray for God to fill the open chair.

D. Develop a list of potential members (use the chart that follows).

Step 2: How to invite new members

A. Develop relationships prior to the group meeting.

B. Explain the vision of your group to the potential member.

C. Ask them to pray about joining the group.

D. Allow them to meet other members of the group before they ever attend a group meeting.

E. Allow them to attend a few meetings before they have to make a final commitment.

Step 3: After new members attend the group

A. Affirm the newcomer and the one who brought him or her.

B. Have everyone briefly retell their own stories.

C. Celebrate what is happening in your group.

D. Don't add people too quickly. Allow the group to assimilate new members and to grow together for a season before inviting additional people.

Note: This is a general process for inviting people to groups. Consult your ministry leaders to determine whether all components of this process apply to your particular kind of group. (For example, seeker groups would use a different method of inviting people into a group, and a task group may have specific guidelines that relate to accomplishing the task.)

Where do I find potential group members?

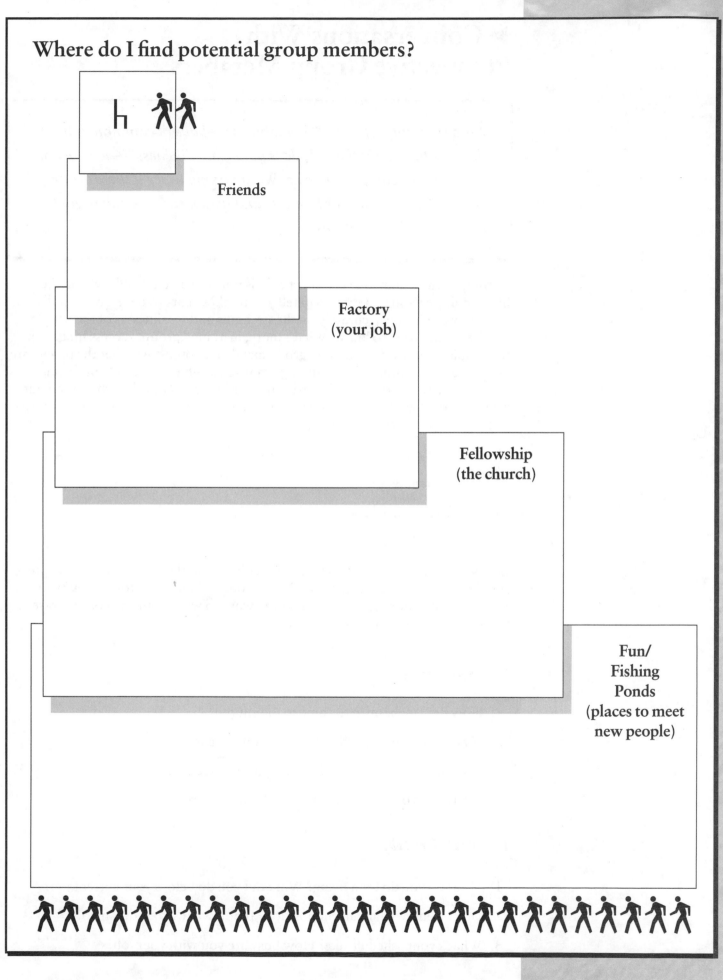

Friends

Factory
(your job)

Fellowship
(the church)

Fun/
Fishing
Ponds
(places to meet
new people)

▶ Conversations With Prospective Group Members

> Affinity *simply refers to "those things we have in common that draw us to one another." It does not mean "likeness"—we are not looking for people just like us. We are trying to see if there are any common experiences or interests that we share so we can begin to develop healthy relationships.*

Getting to know someone in a short time is not easy. Even people who make a living doing this sort of thing will tell you it takes years to develop the skills necessary to pick up accurately on the strengths and weaknesses of the people they're trying to get to know. What's more, in a small group, success hinges on being able to find affinity among group members, not just whether the people are "good people." Although identifying affinity is a subjective and "gut-feeling" type of process, there are some basic questions that can be asked that bring out potential affinity. Questions that get at the heart of whether or not affinity exists can be grouped into four broad areas:

1. Background

2. Job and family

3. Interests and hobbies

4. Spiritual appetite

Below are some examples. As you meet with potential members, don't feel pressured to use all of these questions. Pick the ones you feel comfortable with or that best suit your needs. You might even want to write your own or rephrase these into your own words.

Background

1. How did you happen to come to the church?

2. Where did you go to church before coming here?

3. Are you from the area? Where did you go to school?

4. What was your church background growing up?

Job and family

1. What do you do for a living? What did you do before your current job?

2. Do you enjoy your current position? If not, what's your dream job?

3. What's your schedule like? How busy are you with your job?

4. How long have you been married? Do you have any children? If so, how many?

5. How would you describe your relationship with your spouse? Do you have a date night?

6. What has been the most challenging thing about being married (or single)?

7. What has been the most rewarding thing about being married (or single)?

8. Tell us about your extended family. Do you see your parents much? How many brothers and sisters do you have?

Interests and hobbies

1. What do you like to do with your free time? Do you have any hobbies?

2. What do you like to do when you go out?

3. What do you do to relax?

4. Is there any new sport, activity, or hobby you would like to learn?

Spiritual appetite

1. Have you ever been in a small group before, here or at another church? What did you enjoy about it?

2. Why are you looking to join a small group?

3. How are things going spiritually? How's your walk with God?

4. What do you think you can bring to the lives of others in the small group?

5. What are your expectations for the group? What do you want to see accomplished?

6. Where do you hope to be spiritually at the end of this group?

Please note the design and progression of these questions. Direct inquiries into spiritual specifics or a person's walk with God can be threatening. Consequently, start out asking the simple, nonthreatening questions first. These will loosen them up, and will probably loosen *you* up too!

As the conversation flows, mentally note what you are feeling about the conversation as well as what they are saying. Their body posture, tone of voice, facial gestures, or glances at a spouse, all create reactions within you that can help you see if there is affinity. When some people are getting to know someone else, they err on the side of making judgments too quickly and consequently don't really hear what that person is saying. Others suspend judgment almost to a fault and don't acknowledge their true feelings, possibly missing the fact that they just may not care for the person. Even people with affinity have relational difficulties (think of you and your spouse!). Remember, you are looking for affinity, so don't think you are being "exclusive" (in a negative sense) when you add people to your group with whom you have affinity.

▶Inviting Seekers to Small Groups

Not all groups are prepared to receive seekers. Either the nature of the material being studied or the personalities of members of the group prohibits them from effectively welcoming seekers. If your group desires to invite a seeker, please work with your coach to help prepare your group for this process. For example, you would want to be sensitive in the following areas when inviting seekers to a group meeting or to a social event:

- Focus on the needs of the seeker, not your personal agenda.

- If you discuss a Bible passage, use a version of the Scripture that is seeker friendly.

- Stay away from religious lingo or religious clichés such as "Hallelujah," "Amen, brother!" or terms like, "Lamb of God" or "I'm just trusting in the Blood." Such terminology is unfamiliar to seekers and might scare them away because they will feel like they don't fit in the group.

- Focus on relevancy. Don't get too caught up in theological arguments or distinctions. Stick with the basic truths of Scripture.

- Allow seekers to make comments that might appear strong or opinionated. Don't argue with them. Thank them for their input and help the group respect a seeker's questions or point of view. Listen more than you talk!

- Keep prayers simple. Use normal, conversational language when speaking to God. Help a seeker see that prayer is simply talking with God and not some religious jargon.

These are just a few tips to give you an idea of sensitivities you need to have toward seekers. Again, some seekers should be in a seeker-targeted small group because of the nature of their questions. Others might be welcome in a typical community group. Before inviting seekers to any kind of group, consult your ministry leaders and devise a strategy that would best serve the seeker and the group.

Birthing

Birthing is the term used for the process of group multiplication. The analogy of birthing is appropriate. Birthing involves pain, separation, and some sense of sadness for what has been lost. But it also involves celebration, joy, and appreciation for the new life that has been given and for what has been gained.

Tips to prepare you for birthing

1. Cast a vision for birthing from the onset of the group.

2. Prepare the apprentice for inevitable group leadership.

3. Help the group understand that their purpose is to give life to other groups.

4. Help the group catch a vision for those who are not yet in Christian community.

5. Begin the process of subgrouping several months before birthing. This means that the apprentice leader and the leader each take members of the small group and meet with them separately. This often occurs in two rooms of the same house. However, it allows group members to begin to feel the process of separation from other group members or from the apprentice.

6. The leader and apprentice should each be seeking new apprentices in preparation for birthing.

7. New apprentices and members should be brought to the subgroups.

8. Begin meeting as subgroups for the entire meeting time.

9. At the time of birth, celebrate the beginning of a new group.

Day of Birth

Like any birthday, this is a time for celebration. As the new group begins to finally separate from the existing group, it's time to gather together and celebrate new life. Here are some ways to celebrate the joys and experience the sadness of a group birth on the day of birth.

1. Have a time of celebration for the birth.

2. Hold a time of prayer as you commission and bless the new group.

3. Recognize and affirm the new leadership in each group.

4. Allow members to express their feelings of celebration and sadness.

5. Plan a time when the two groups will come together again to reunite (probably in four to six weeks).

6. Have a time of communion together and share the victories and blessings of the previous group.

7. Spend time praying about the future of both groups and what God might do to help each grow spiritually and numerically.

8. Have each member write a letter to the rest of the group expressing their feelings of thankfulness and respect.

9. Take pictures or videos of the groups as you prepare to birth.

10. Set a schedule for a few planned social events together in the future so that the group reunites on a regular basis.

Types of Births

Below you'll find a chart explaining four types of birthing possibilities.

Birthing New Groups

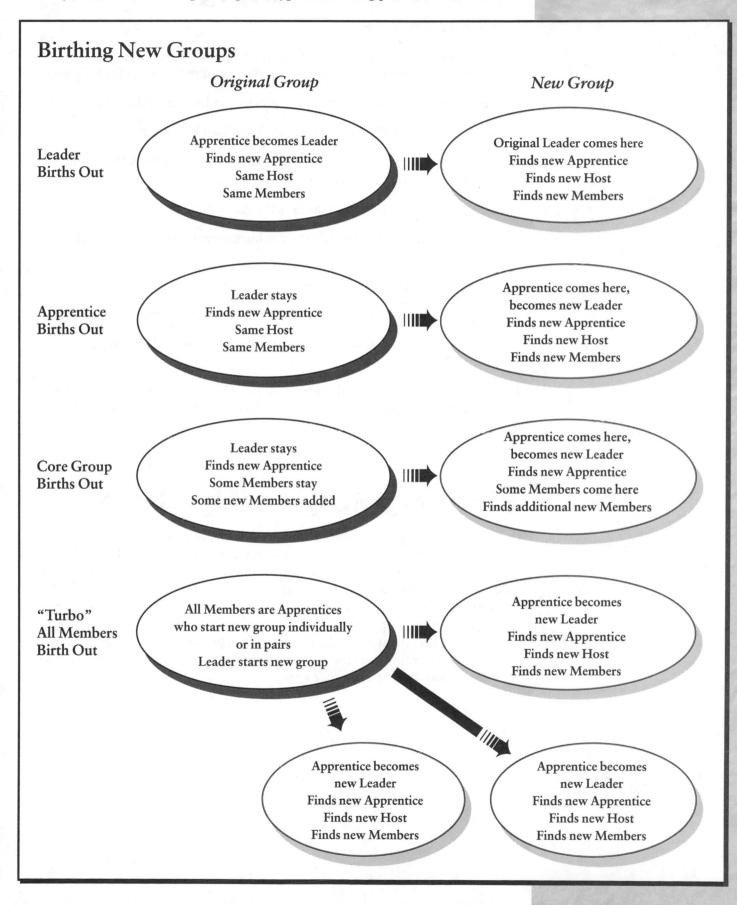

Original Group   *New Group*

Leader Births Out

Apprentice becomes Leader
Finds new Apprentice
Same Host
Same Members

→

Original Leader comes here
Finds new Apprentice
Finds new Host
Finds new Members

Apprentice Births Out

Leader stays
Finds new Apprentice
Same Host
Same Members

→

Apprentice comes here,
becomes new Leader
Finds new Apprentice
Finds new Host
Finds new Members

Core Group Births Out

Leader stays
Finds new Apprentice
Some Members stay
Some new Members added

→

Apprentice comes here,
becomes new Leader
Finds new Apprentice
Some Members come here
Finds additional new Members

"Turbo" All Members Birth Out

All Members are Apprentices
who start new group individually
or in pairs
Leader starts new group

→

Apprentice becomes
new Leader
Finds new Apprentice
Finds new Host
Finds new Members

Apprentice becomes
new Leader
Finds new Apprentice
Finds new Host
Finds new Members

Apprentice becomes
new Leader
Finds new Apprentice
Finds new Host
Finds new Members

Reducing the Trauma of Birthing

To reduce the trauma of birthing:

1. Talk about the goal of birthing from the beginning. Talk about birthing often and optimistically. If birthing is sprung on the group, they will resist.

2. Set up the apprentice to succeed by giving him/her leadership opportunities.

3. Honor "core units" of two or three who cannot be split up.

4. Allow for "gestation" by letting the "baby" develop an identity within the "mother" *(meet in separate rooms in the same house for a period of time)*.

5. Have a "birth party" when the actual birth occurs.

6. Allow for "nursing"; periodically getting the two groups together after the birth.

7. Encourage grief work.

8. Prepare to strategically add new members to your group.

9. Celebrate "grandchildren"—groups developed out of the group you birthed!

10. Small group leaders should meet with individual group members after a group has birthed in order to process the birth on a one-to-one basis.

Birthing Follow-Up Care

Once the new group has birthed out of the existing group, the existing group should spend a meeting or two processing what has taken place. This will help groups officially separate and yet express feelings and sadness about the birthing process. Also, you should begin to pray about new members for the group. Take a few meetings to reorient as a group, but then begin the process of opening the chair and inviting people into this new community. Remember, this group is now a new group, because it is not the same as it was before. Leaders must give particular attention to group members during this time, as they may be experiencing feelings of sadness, frustration, or loss.

Resources

Commonly Asked Questions about Multiplying Your Ministry

Q *How long should it take for my group to birth?*

A Groups birth at various rates. The key to birthing is not the number of meetings as much as it is the preparation of the apprentice leader. Groups are ready to birth when apprentices are ready to lead and have identified a new apprentice for themselves. On average, a typical group should birth every 12–18 months. But birthing will vary by ministry and by group depending on how often the group meets, the readiness of the apprentice, and the nature of the ministry.

Q *What if our birth is not successful?*

A From time to time some births are not successful. That is, it is difficult for the new group to get started. In such cases, work closely with your ministry leaders and determine what is the best solution. Things in life don't always work out perfectly, and the same is true of small groups. Spend time in prayer asking God to give you wisdom for the situation.

Q *What if I want seekers in the group and the group doesn't want them?*

A The best way to destroy a group is to bring seekers into it when the group is not prepared to receive them. This could also seriously damage a seeker's opinion of Christianity. If you, as a leader, are very anxious to work with seekers (and feel gifted in this area), then you should think about developing an apprentice who can take over your group as you birth out to lead a seeker-targeted group.

Q *How important is evangelism for small groups?*

A Evangelism is an important part of the normal Christian life and, therefore, is important in small groups as well. However, that does not mean that each group becomes an evangelistic small group. As mentioned above, some groups do well to invite seekers and can handle them with the appropriate care and concern. Other groups are not prepared to do so. The important thing is that each member of the small group understands how to effectively explain the Gospel and "owns" the value of evangelism. The group may simply decide to pray for and support one another in individual evangelistic efforts with neighbors or coworkers. Take the *Becoming a Contagious Christian* training course and learn how to best spread the message of Christianity based on each person's own personality and gifts.

Q *What if I have trouble finding members for my small group?*

A First, talk to your ministry leaders. Your ministry may have "fishing pond" events where people seeking group life will gather. If you make the effort to attend such events, you will have a good chance of meeting some people ("fishing") who would fit into your group. Take advantage of the events sponsored by your ministry for meeting new people. In addition, talk to your division leader or ministry director and ask if there are any persons who have contacted them and are interested in small group life.

Q *How is affinity determined?*

A The word *affinity* does not mean "likeness." Affinity simply means there is enough in common between two people that a relationship is likely to occur. This common ground may be life-stage, number of children in your family, age, similar ministry interests, similar work interests, similar problems or needs, or similar hobbies and interests. Affinity is not a principle that is designed to exclude people. Rather, it is a principle to honor because it exists in reality. People tend to organize themselves around those with whom they feel comfortable. While it is admirable to want to reach out to all people, it is important to recognize that people tend to "connect" based on affinity.

Q *What about those people who have trouble connecting to the church and don't seem to have affinity with others?*

A There are always a few people who have difficulty developing relationships. This may be for a variety of reasons. Perhaps they don't know anyone because they just moved into the area, or perhaps they've had difficulty with social skills or are very introverted. This does not mean they can't participate in small groups. Talk with your ministry leaders to find ways to incorporate such people into your group. As a church, try to provide enough events and activities within each ministry so that different kinds of people can find a place to belong. You don't want anyone to fall through the cracks. If you know of someone who has difficulty connecting to a small group, contact your ministry leaders and discuss a strategy for helping them get involved.

Additional Resources

Becoming a Contagious Christian (book and training materials) by Bill Hybels and Mark Mittelberg (Zondervan)

Evangelism as a Lifestyle by Jim Peterson (NavPress)
This is a great book for helping people develop relational skills as lifestyle evangelists. Peterson's book discusses a process to help people build relationships in which they can ultimately share their faith.

Out of the Saltshaker by Rebecca Pippert (InterVarsity)
This is another great book for how to be salt and light in the world so as to impact people with the Gospel.

Prepare Your Church for the Future by Carl George (Revell)
Carl George discusses ministry multiplication in chapters 5 and 9, where he gives a good picture of the birthing process. This would be helpful reading for any groups preparing to birth.

Part Eight

Starting Small Groups in Your Church

Getting Started

"How do we get started?" is a question many people ask after they see the value of doing ministry together in groups. It is not difficult to get a few small groups started, but it takes wisdom and planning to prepare for success. Many ministries don't plan for success. The question you must address is, "What do you do when small groups work and more people want to be in them and leaders need additional training?"

There is a big difference between starting "small groups" and starting "a ministry based on small groups." Refer to the introduction to jog your memory about the difference between a church "with" small groups and a church "of" small groups.

If you want to get a single small group started, refer to Part 4, where we discussed the essential foundations of a group: having a vision, setting goals, forming a covenant, and agreeing on values. Part 7 will help you find new members, and Part 3 will help you in identifying a developing an apprentice leader, someone you can disciple into leadership.

But if you want to build a church or an entire ministry using small groups as the foundation and main vehicle for accomplishing your mission, there are many more things to consider.

Eight Key Questions

Often churches eager to develop a new ministry focus primarily on the future—the vision, outcomes, staffing, budgeting, materials, and all the other resources necessary to "get the job done." But before moving ahead to consider the kind of church you'd like to be, it is essential to have a clear understanding of the kind of church you are. Here are some key questions to consider:

▶From Where Have We Come?

Trace your history to clarify your heritage, past values, attendance trends, and the stages through which your ministry has progressed over the years. Take some time to evaluate your history in light of some of these categories:

- Teaching topics
- Staff changes
- Major events in the church
- Major events in the world around you
- Changes in demographics
- Crises and tragedies
- Styles of ministry
- Budgets
- Previous reactions to change
- Ministries started and ended

This exercise will be of great benefit to understanding who you are as a church because it will provide a meaningful review of your past, allow you to learn from successes and failures, and bring newer members up to speed with some of your more seasoned veterans. It also will allow you to celebrate what God has done so that you can begin to pray about what He will do in the future. Have older members tell stories about each of the phases your church has gone through. You will honor your past and create a greater sense of unity.

▶Where Are We Today?

Now begin dialogue about present ministries, staff, vision, and effectiveness. This is simply an extension of the previous exercise. What is it that you are doing right now as a church and how do you gauge your success in doing what God is asking you to do? What is your present structure or model for ministry (large worship gatherings, Sunday school, adult Bible fellowships, classes, small groups, informal groups, associations, et cetera)? Why do you have each of these ministries? Are they effective?

▶What Are Our Core Values?

Every church has a set values by which it functions. Sometimes these are well understood and clearly articulated; in other churches, they are unwritten but understood by insiders. For a church to move ahead toward the process of implementing a small group model, you must first determine what values are central to your ministry. Then you can determine whether small groups will reinforce those values.

Some values that merit discussion by your leaders are:

- **Building relationships.** Caring about others and seeking to know and understand them.

- **Loving lost people.** Since all people matter to God, lost people are close to His heart.

- **Truth-telling.** Graciously and lovingly speaking truth to one another, not hiding issues, harboring resentments, spreading gossip, or avoiding healthy conflict.

- **Mutual ministry.** Everyone shares together in ministry; it is not for just a few paid professionals.

- **Accountability.** Committing to one another to practice integrity and moral discipline, allowing a brother or sister in Christ to inquire about each other's conduct and progress in carrying out responsibilities or behaviors.

- **Commitment.** Following through and owning responsibility for the mission.

Whatever you choose as core values for your church, be certain they are biblically based, well articulated, agreed upon by all senior leadership, taught, and modeled.

Now you can determine whether shaping a ministry around small groups will help you instill and uphold such values.

▶ Who Influences Decisions in Our Church?

Since this small group ministry is going to be a major initiative of your church, you want to make sure the vision and values are understood and embraced by as many key decision influencers as possible. These people are those who are often sought after when considering any major decision at the church. In some cases, you will need their approval (elders, special committees, boards). In other cases, you will need their agreement (key volunteers, major donors, long-term members).

Caution: We are not talking about politics here. But you do need to be wise about change, and the way it takes place. If certain people tend to influence decisions, direction, and strategy in your church, it is wise to communicate with them, respect them, and seek to gain their blessing on your efforts. You must go about this with absolute integrity and without manipulation.

Some of these people are not in formal positions of authority in the church, but may be married to people who are. Or perhaps they helped start the church through their generosity and care deeply about its direction. Bring these people into your process as counselors and advisers. Seek out their wisdom, listen to their concerns, give attention to the problems they raise, thank them for caring enough to work it through with you.

Also realize that no matter what you do, some people just won't get on board. Be sure God is calling you and others to make the move to small groups, because if you are not sure, you will give up in the face of some disagreement or adversity. If it is the consensus of the senior leadership to move ahead, do so. Continue to love and communicate with those who will not support your efforts. Invite their critique. But also continue to fulfill your God-given mission. Change always creates some level of conflict or disagreement. Expect it, prepare for it, pray through it, and move ahead wisely.

► How Will We Craft and Articulate the Vision to Our Key Leadership?

Once you have consensus on the general direction and values, set out to get a vision statement in writing. This will keep you focused and provide a tool for articulating your vision to those whom you lead. Include the biblical basis for your vision and values. For a sample, refer to the Willow Creek Statement in Part 1. Take your time crafting your vision statement. Include many people's input and feedback. You want consensus from a large group of leaders so that as many people as possible "own" the vision.

As you go through this process, remember to consider what you want to avoid and what you want to preserve before addressing what you want to achieve. People feel safer talking about the future after you have assured them you want to keep worthwhile values from the past and are concerned about avoiding unnecessary problems in the future.

► What are Potential Resources and Possible Barriers?

What resources exist for you to implement small groups? Some may have to be developed along the way, but below are some categories to consider. Each of these categories may be a resource or a barrier depending on whether you have sufficient amounts of each.

Leaders or potential leaders

Finances—budgeted or outside donors

Training and curriculum materials

Audio-visual equipment for training and for presentations

Staff—amount of time each staff member can devote to group development

Consultants—experts from within the congregation and outside it

A forum for dialogue and exchange—a regular place or meeting to evaluate results and handle difficulties

Facilities for training and for meetings—off campus is best, but some groups will need to meet on-site

► How Should We Repurpose or Rearrange Existing Meetings to Include Group Life?

Depending on your existing meeting and service schedule, you may want to leverage those meetings for training and vision-casting. Many of your volunteer leaders and potential leaders are already committed to the church in various activities. Adding more training events and meetings to their schedules could overwhelm them.

Here are a few suggestions to help you:

1. Add training or short meetings to existing services. Ask child-care workers to work an extra 20–30 minutes one Sunday morning service per month, and have small group leaders come for training during that time. This will allow you to deliver very focused, specific training and to communicate important information to your leaders without asking them to make another trip to church.

2. Change the focus of a Sunday evening service to accommodate small group issues and leadership topics. A sermon series could focus on any of the following topics:

    *   Building lasting relationships

    *   Truth-telling

    *   Handling conflict

    *   Making fully devoted followers

    *   Using your gifts to impact others

    *   The "one anothers" of the New Testament

    *   Intercessory prayer

    These topics will benefit the entire body, but leaders will be able to take the topics and apply them in terms of their groups. In essence, it will provide a level of skill training. Provide a handout for leaders that can be used in their groups later that week.

3. Redesign some of the Sunday school classes around leadership training issues. Target a class for leaders of groups. Have leaders bring potential leaders to the class. Run the class as a "model group" as well as a teaching and training event. This kind of a class will have additional impact if the senior pastor or other key leader teaches it from time to time.

4. Add or include a group time or community-building time to existing board and committee meetings. This will help senior leadership model group life for the congregation, give them a taste of group life, and help them build a stronger team. As these men and women see the value of group life and how it can enhance their efforts, they will be more supportive of the church moving in the direction of groups as a means of doing ministry.

▶ What Are the Implications for Our Staff?

Initially, if a church is committed to becoming a church of small groups, each staff member will have to direct time and energy toward the development of groups. This can be achieved by *growing* into small group ministry, not *going* into small group ministry.

Each year for 3–5 years replace 20 percent of a staff member's job description with small group development responsibility. It looks like this:

Year 1–80% current, 20% groups

Year 2–60% current, 40% groups

Year 3–40% current, 60% groups

This pattern allows a gradual move into small group emphasis by each staff member. It does, however, assume a few key factors:

- Twenty percent of current responsibilities must be dropped so that time can be spent building groups. So this can take place, you must help staff prioritize ministry responsibilities.

- Volunteers may have to be recruited to be part of the staff team. This is usually very healthy since many staff view themselves as doers of ministry instead of releasing ministry to others.

- As small group involvement increases, staff will understand how mobilizing groups into areas of vital ministry actually helps get more done than if the staff member were doing it alone. Groups become a way of doing the ministry tasks that the church must accomplish while paying attention to the building of little communities where life change can occur.

Phasing In the Small Group Ministry

Four Phases

Many churches, including Willow Creek, made some mistakes by moving into the small group model too quickly. Fortunately, we were able to make adjustments, but some ministries failed because churches decided to *go* into small groups instead of *grow* into them. Pulpit announcements, launching too many groups too soon, not planning for success, and not allowing time for the training and development of future leaders can stifle attempts at developing groups. It is better to move in phases, if possible.

▶ The Modeling Phase

In the Modeling Phase, church leaders (preferably including the senior pastor) lead one or two small groups. These groups should be filled with other potential leaders, people who have never experienced a vital small group, and a few people who have had less-than-desirable group experiences. Take the time necessary to model the vision and values you want for these groups. Experiment, take risks, invite feedback, and make changes. Along the way, you may have to break a few paradigms.

Each person has a different picture come to mind when they hear the words "small groups." Here are a few:

1. **Content-intensive Bible study:** Groups filled with informational discussions about Bible doctrines, interpretations of the second coming, and a focus on being right. Lots of notebooks, reference books, Greek studies, word study books, and other materials.

2. **Therapy group:** Groups where people come just to get their own "stuff" fixed or discussed. Little interest in giving to others, studying the Word, or growing spiritually.

3. **Social gathering:** Groups where people hang out together, have refreshments, share a few prayer requests, and plan the next event. The focus is on Betty's new drapes, Bob's new car, Alaine's new roommate, and the latest box office hits.

4. **Religious discussion:** Groups where people debate lots of religious issues but never get at the truth of Scripture. Discussions focus on near death experiences, angelic revelations, what all religions have in common, and the latest spiritual experience of a member.

The above misperceptions is why modeling is so critical. Regardless of someone's background, they need to see exactly what you expect from a small group. Emphasize the distinctives your church wants to highlight. Show people how certain small group values are lived out as you

- fill the open chair by inviting newcomers

- train your apprentice leader(s)

- reach out to seekers who don't know Christ

- prepare to birth new groups from your group

- handle conflict and struggles

- celebrate life change

- have fun

- bring variety to a meeting

- serve together

The very fact that you are in the process of developing a group will earn you the respect of others and the right to champion the vision.

▶ The Turbo Phase

This phase is sometimes combined with the Modeling Phase. The difference is that turbo groups are filled almost exclusively with apprentice leaders. A group in Turbo Phase is a turbocharged small group designed to intentionally develop and release leaders, thus starting several new groups at once as it births. The group leader trains apprentices for a season by modeling and teaching the group values and group process. At the end of the turbo group, everyone "births" and forms their own groups. We recommend this phase include at least 10–15 meetings. A turbo group should allow apprentices to

- practice leadership skills

- find their own apprentice(s)

- invite people to the group

- subgroup into groups of three to five for prayer and leadership development

- observe and practice healthy group dynamics

Turbo groups are great for speeding up the process of leadership development. But be careful to take the time necessary to actually *develop* these potential leaders, giving them the experience they need along the way. If this process is accelerated too quickly, you can be in big trouble when you turn these leaders loose. Remember, lots of future group members' lives are at stake. Taking time to train leader's sufficiently in the beginning will avoid a lot of problems down the road.

▶ The Pilot Phase

With the Pilot Phase, all members know they are in a pilot group experience. You start by asking a handful of well-trained leaders to lead small groups for 12–16 meetings. (It is good to go for 12–16 meetings so that groups get beyond the "honeymoon" stage and have some conflict.) After the final meeting, the groups pause for evaluation and feedback. Pilot groups still model and teach the core values you have decided upon, but they are not specifically designed to birth until feedback has been gathered.

The Pilot Phase is a great time to experiment. You have permission to fail because everyone knows it is a pilot and that they're going to have important impact in any changes that need to be made. During this phase you will want to meet very regularly with leaders. And leaders must be willing to push the groups a little. Because the number of meetings is limited, you want to make sure leaders use it well.

▶ The Start-Up Phase

Once a church has done some of the groundwork listed above, it's time to launch the small group ministry more broadly. But this does not mean it is time to "go public." A premature announcement inviting everyone to join a small group is not a good idea. Not only will it create ministry chaos for the staff, it will cause you to put people into leadership prematurely and will frustrate members who try to get into groups but cannot find one that has room for them.

In the Start-up Phase you are still operating mostly by word of mouth to advertise the small group ministry. Leaders and apprentices (having completed a turbo- or model-group experience) are now asked to recruit members to their groups. Each leader and apprentice team will recruit at least six people before beginning a group.

Before entering the Start-up Phase, make sure the leadership training process is firmly in place. Without this, you are setting leaders up for failure. Pay attention to these details:

1. **Location.** Where is the best place for a creative, dynamic training session?

2. **Time.** What is the best time for your leaders? Will you offer multiple sessions for them to choose from?

3. **Materials.** Don't give leaders poor quality materials to pass out. If you expect their best, give them your best. Use a good printer and copier, even if you have to do it somewhere other than the church.

4. **Duration.** This depends on how often leaders gather for training. If every six weeks, then take about two hours, provide a snack, and include huddle time with their coaches (overseers) or staff. If weekly, keep it to 30–40 minutes.

5. **Senior leadership.** Involve the pastor and elders often so that leaders know they are at the center of what's happening. Value leaders by investing in them and providing them with current, up-to-date information about the church and ministry efforts.

6. **Coaches.** Begin to identify potential "shepherds of the shepherds" who will care for leaders as your ministry grows. Don't overlook this, or you will have too many leaders under one person's span of care.

Going Public

If you have successfully completed the phases above and are preparing to develop coaches for your leaders, then you are ready to go public with the ministry. Granted, many may already know about it. (Hopefully they have been hearing stories from pilot groups and small group leaders and can't wait to get into a group!) Before actually announcing that the church is now going full swing into a small group ministry that encompasses the entire church, make sure you have considered these issues:

1. Are there enough open chairs in existing groups to accommodate new people?

2. Are you identifying coaches who will provide care and support to small group leaders? Remember, to honor span of care for coaches, you need one coach for every five small groups. Staff and elders can initially serve as coaches, but ideally you want coaches to "come up through the system" after having led and birthed a group themselves.

3. Are you prepared to look for new leaders among those who express an interest in joining a group? Many good leaders are reluctant to come forward to lead. Be ready to challenge them.

4. Do you have a "holding tank" ready if you are overwhelmed with requests? These are classes where people can experience a small group format before actually joining a group. These classes allow you time to find some more leaders and provide a place for people who are waiting to get into groups.

5. Are you prepared to pay the price? Your church will never be the same. There will be great challenges and issues to address (most of which are the products of success). Stay committed to the vision. Everyone in key positions of staff and volunteer leadership must be "on board" before you launch.

Developing Small Group Leader Training

Leader training is key to the long term success of small group ministry. Your ministry reproduces itself through the ongoing development of leaders, so those leaders had better be equipped.

There are two primary ways in which small group leaders are trained for ministry—decentralized training which takes place outside the formal training classes, and centralized training provided by trainers. Let's talk about these two methods.

Decentralized Training

▶On-The-Job Training

Apprentice leaders learn by observing and experimenting in the context of real group life. This can be the most effective kind of training. Its effectiveness depends largely on the relationship between leader and apprentice, and between apprentice and coach. Coaches who visit groups can provide tips and encouragement to rising apprentice leaders, and leaders can walk alongside apprentices to give them feedback, allow them opportunities to lead meetings, and encourage apprentices as they grow into leadership roles.

▶Huddle-Based Training

The huddle is an opportunity for leaders to gain informal, need-based training from coaches. In a huddle, coaches (who in most cases have discernment and greater experience) provide counsel and mentoring to leaders under their care. Tips and ideas are exchanged, problems are addressed, and resources are provided.

▶ Ministry-Based Training

In churches with multiple ministry areas (singles, youth, music, men's), those ministries will provide targeted, focused training that has application to the unique components of that ministry. For example, the youth ministry director may decide to bring in a youth specialist from the congregation or the community to train small group leaders to better understand the needs and struggles of youth in today's culture.

▶ Self-Directed Learning

Leaders take advantage of tapes and books and other handouts from a "leader's library," a place where they can access information and resources for training.

Centralized Training

Centralized, staff-directed training takes place on campus, where leaders can gather with staff for specific instruction. This is an ideal setting for role play, demonstration of skills, vision casting, case study, and video presentation. Most centralized training should take place at the beginning stages of leadership. After that, leaders will move to more decentralized methods where they can self-select the learning and training they need.

If you use church-based, staff-directed training sessions, make sure you create an exciting and dynamic environment. Use lectures minimally but effectively. Keep the training interactive.

▶ Questions to Answer Before Conducting a Church-Based Training Event

Is it personal?

Many training programs are designed around a curriculum. But we feel training programs must be designed around the leader. Begin with a definition or picture of what kind of person a successful small group leader needs to be. Consider both character and skill development. Once you have listed a set of characteristics and skills, identify a set of absolute minimums—core skills and behaviors without which small group leaders cannot or should not lead a group. Then begin to develop materials and training guidelines for these core skills, shaping them into your required or foundational training for all new leaders.

Key Question: Is our training material designed to benefit the learner or the teacher?

Is it biblical?

Because we are working with small groups as a structure within the church, the temptation is to focus on group dynamics and skills. These are essential and should never be dismissed as optional. However, do not neglect the incorporation of solid biblical material and teaching for your leaders. The Scriptures are fundamental for giving your people a Christ-centered vision for leadership, relationships, community, and shepherding. Use key passages like Ezekiel 34, Matthew 10, Luke 10, and John 10 for shepherding and leadership development. Help your people understand their role as ministers of the Gospel using Ephesians 4, and of the need for humility and servanthood using John 13 and Philippians 2.

Use the Bible to transform leaders, not simply inform them. Cast a biblically-based vision for leadership and present biblical values and guidelines for ministry. Combine that with skill training for caregiving, conducting life changing meetings, launching creative Bible discussions, listening, intercessory and group prayer, and spiritual gifts assessment and deployment, and you will have a powerful training program.

Key question: Will leaders feel they have been fed and encouraged from the Word?

Is it developmental?

Design and organize your training and teaching in such a way that leaders feel they are making progress. In the early days, Willow Creek provided a menu-based training program. Leaders took what they needed to help them with their groups. But we failed to organize it in a way that not only met felt needs (like solving group conflict) but also taught them in areas of growth (like becoming a shepherd). The "menu" method can only provide options—it will not help a leader determine which is the best choice.

A developmental approach not only offers an array of training materials and support, it provides a plan for leaders that helps them determine goals and guidelines for personal growth. Since not everyone is the same, the plan must be flexible and yet include much of the basic training all leaders need. After the required foundational training, provide leaders with a system of training that helps them make wise choices. At Willow Creek, we rely on the small group coaches to work with their leaders using a leadership development plan to recommend training options for their people. This accountability and mutual support provides a framework for choosing and using the appropriate training depending on each stage of group development.

Key question: How will our leaders grow as a result of this training?

Is it inspirational?

Some training can be like going to the dentist. It's difficult, takes a lot of time, and the main reason you go is because you have to. (Your teeth will eventually fall out if you don't.) Personally, I have begun to enjoy going to my dentist. He's friendly, spends focused time with me, recommends reasonable steps I can take to keep hygienically healthy, asks about my personal life and family, and always greets me enthusiastically. Training can be that way too.

Remember, most people who lead groups have already been through some type of training for their jobs—and a lot of it resembled a talking head telling them information and giving out a lot of handouts for three-ring binders that will sit on a shelf (next to the other nine binders from other training programs). So "training" is often perceived as tedious.

But imagine coming into a room that is well-lit and decorated creatively with colored papers or balloons. Mints and candies are on all the tables and light refreshments are available. Be creative with the set-up of your presentation. Instead of simply standing behind a podium or in front of a chalk board, try using a table with your materials on it. Use overheads, video, flip charts, and slides. Have fun. Incorporate some creative icebreakers and relationship-building games. Speak with enthusiasm and passion. All this will help create and inspiring and motivating atmosphere that says "This isn't business as usual."

Key Question: Will leaders be motivated by the training?

Is it relational?

Much training methodology is designed around the higher educational models of learning, namely, the classroom experience. Relational training involves participatory learning. Groups and teams are more conducive to experiential learning modes that allow learners to experiment with new skills, gain feedback, process information with other learners, and develop peer-level relationships with other leaders. It takes more work to build training into a group-based design, but the results are worth it.

Key Question: Is group interaction and learning taking place?

Is it applicational?

Does the training experience easily lend itself to immediate and fruitful application in the next group meeting? Remember, leaders are often thinking about the issues immediately facing their groups. Like most adult learners, they are not interested in training that might help them eight months from now. It must apply to group life today or it will not seem relevant.

In foundational or required introductory training, it is fine to provide members with a broad array of basic training. But focus on core essentials and do not overwhelm them with "all the training they'll ever need" in the introductory session.

Key Question: Will leaders use it this week?

Is it transformational?

Many training processes focus on skill acquisition or the communication of information. But the ultimate goal of training is a transformed leader—not just a more skilled leader or a more knowledgeable leader. Training processes and events must change the heart of a leader so that the leader becomes an agent of the work of the Holy Spirit. If the previous six questions have been successfully addressed, the transformation question almost answers itself. In other words, if training is personal, biblical, developmental, inspirational, relational, applicational, it will be transformational.

The goal of the trainer is to provide a feedback loop to discern whether any change has indeed taken place. This can be done in several ways. First, as coaches or overseers visit groups and work with small group leaders, they may be able to discern changes in behavior and attitude directly related to a training experience. Second, ask leaders for feedback on any given training experience. Immediate reaction-level feedback can provide some indication of change, or a simple questionnaire or feedback form accomplishes this as well. Focus groups can also be helpful. Schedule focus groups for six to ten weeks after the training experience and ask participants to reflect on their experience and how it has (or has not) affected group life and leadership. (This will also give you a feel for how much material or skills leaders actually retain or use.) All of these types of feedback will dramatically improve how and what you deliver in training experiences for your people.

Key Question: Did learners actually change behavior or attitudes because of this training?

Points to Remember

- Keep training sessions focused on one or two key skills

- Use all the creativity at your disposal

- Always start and end on time

- Gain feedback from learners

- Make training accessible and enjoyable

With these guidelines and principles in action, you will have a quality and effective training process in place.

Evaluating Your Small Group Ministry

Checkpoints Along the Way

Every ministry must pause and ask the questions, "Are we really effective? Is our ministry making an impact? Are we really stewarding the resources God has given us with wisdom? Are our people growing to be more like Christ, acting as He would in their place?"

►How Is My Group Doing?

In starting and developing a ministry that uses small groups as the primary vehicle for delivering care, truth, and service to the body of Christ, there are some tools for evaluating the growth and progress of members and leaders.

For example, at Willow Creek we have designed the Shepherding Plan found in Part 6 of this book. The Shepherding Plan is designed as a leadership development and discipleship tool for group leaders. The Five G's (grace, growth, group, gifts, good stewardship) provide a grid for giving feedback to group members. We ask the question, "How is our group doing in _____?", filling the blank in with each one of the Five G's. Using the Shepherding Plan on a quarterly basis allows us to take a "snapshot" of the group and provide members with meaningful feedback about their growth in Christ. It can be used in one-on-one settings, but is primarily designed to evaluate the group as a whole.

►How Am I Doing as a Leader?

In Part 5 of this book you will find a Leader Feedback and Development form. You could design your own or simply copy this one. If you really want to know how your leaders are doing, then do two things:

1. Visit their groups three to four times per year.

2. Give group members the Leader Feedback and Development form and ask them to provide meaningful, constructive feedback for their leaders.

The process of evaluation and feedback is scary for many people. It is important to convey that your goal is development, not criticism. If groups can do this on their own, it becomes a community-building experience. Leaders hear what is working and what needs attention, and can be affirmed and yet challenged. Leaders should discuss the feedback with their coach who will be able to provide them with suggestions and encouragement.

▶ How Are Our Meetings Going?

Another form we have used at Willow Creek is the Touching Base form in Part 5. Again, you will probably want to design your own, but this kind of form will give your staff a comprehensive overview of the ministry at your church in a given month or quarter. Ask leaders to fill it out every month at their huddle meeting and give it to their coach. It will become an ongoing "journal" of the group, a kind of group history. This information can be compiled to give a picture of the ministry at any given time. Though numbers certainly don't tell the whole story, they can be an important indicator of group health and progress. The Touching Base form will also reveal trends in the ministry. Are there enough apprentices being developed? How often are groups being visited? How often are groups using the open chair to invite new people? How many groups have stopped and why?

In addition to using these two forms, we recommend getting some discussion groups together once or twice a year. Gather a few members from each of your small groups and ask them how things are going. (Make sure a non-staff person facilitates this discussion. People will be more open if staff or their small group leader is not present.) Also, you will want to gather leaders and coaches together for their own focus groups. They will provide you with valuable feedback, giving a clear picture of reality. Allow them opportunities in their groups or huddles to discuss their "sticking points." Listen to them without being defensive or judgmental. Aim for understanding and clarity.

Most importantly, make changes or improvements based on the leaders' feedback, and let them know it! Sometimes it's easy to gather data or information and never tell people how we used it. As a result, people feel devalued and unheard. But if you can show people that their input matters—that it has influence and is heard—you will gain their respect and loyalty. Your leaders don't expect you to be perfect, but they do want to know you are listening and working to develop them as people.

If you don't take the time to ask these questions, you will never know how your ministry is really doing. You may resort to pretending all is well. As a result, groups become less effective, newcomers remain unconnected, disciples are not made, improvements are not implemented, and lives go unchanged. Ultimately, the church—the bride of Christ—is inadequately shepherded. All because we are unwilling to ask hard questions and make necessary changes.

Resources

Commonly Asked Questions about Starting Small Groups

Q *How much will it cost to launch this ministry?*

A It depends on whether you want to build a church on small groups or simply add groups to your program. We have found it worth the investment to allocate significant resources to the training, development, and growth of group life throughout the church. Be prepared to change your budget, staffing, and support systems to make small groups productive.

Additional Resources

The Change Agent by Lyle Schaller (Abingdon)
> Recently revised, this is a classic and thorough book on change in the church. A must-read if you're serious about major transitions.

The Coming Church Revolution by Carl George and Warren Bird (Revell)
> George's chapters on change and transition are valuable for the development of a new small group ministry.

An Introduction to Helping Adults Learn and Change by Russel D. Robinson (Bible Study Press)
> A great, concise resource for designing adult education programs. Includes everything from teaching tips to classroom design to motivation principles.

Index

WILLOW CREEK

RESOURCES

This resource was created to serve you.

It is just one of many ministry tools that are part of the Willow Creek Resources® line, published by the Willow Creek Association together with Zondervan Publishing House. The Willow Creek Association was created in 1992 to serve a rapidly growing number of churches from all across the denominational spectrum that are committed to helping unchurched people become fully devoted followers of Christ. There are now more than 2,500 WCA member churches worldwide.

The Willow Creek Association links like-minded leaders with each other and with strategic vision, information, and resources in order to build prevailing churches. Here are some of the ways it does that:

• **Church Leadership Conferences**—3 1/2 -day events, held at Willow Creek Community Church in South Barrington, IL, that are being used by God to help church leaders find new and innovative ways to build prevailing churches that reach unchurched people.

• **The Leadership Summit**—a once-a-year event designed to increase the leadership effectiveness of pastors, ministry staff, volunteer church leaders, and Christians in business.

• **Willow Creek Resources®**—to provide churches with a trusted channel of ministry resources in areas of leadership, evangelism, spiritual gifts, small groups, drama, contemporary music, and more. For more information, call Willow Creek Resources® at 800/876-7335. Outside the US call 610/532-1249.

• *WCA News*—a bimonthly newsletter to inform you of the latest trends, resources, and information on WCA events from around the world.

• *The Exchange*—our classified ads publication to assist churches in recruiting key staff for ministry positions.

• **The Church Associates Directory**—to keep you in touch with other WCA member churches around the world.

• *WillowNet*—an Internet service that provides access to hundreds of Willow Creek messages, drama scripts, songs, videos and multimedia suggestions. The system allows users to sort through these elements and download them for a fee.

• *Defining Moments*—a monthly audio journal for church leaders, in which Lee Strobel asks Bill Hybels and other Christian leaders probing questions to help you discover biblical principles and transferable strategies to help maximize your church's potential.

For conference and membership information please write or call:

Willow Creek Association
P.O. Box 3188
Barrington, IL 60011-3188
ph: (847) 765-0070
fax: (847) 765-5046
www.willowcreek.org

0597